Disabled Christianity

Disabled Christianity

◆

Recognizing and Cultivating a Desperate Dependence upon God

Aaron J. Gunzer

iUniverse, Inc.
New York Lincoln Shanghai

Disabled Christianity
Recognizing and Cultivating a Desperate Dependence upon God

iUniverse books may be ordered through booksellers or by contacting:

iUniverse
2021 Pine Lake Road, Suite 100
Lincoln, NE 68512
www.iuniverse.com
1-800-Authors (1-800-288-4677)

Because of the dynamic nature of the Internet, any Web addresses or links contained in this book may have changed since publication and may no longer be valid.

ISBN: 978-0-595-45481-5 (pbk)
ISBN: 978-0-595-89793-3 (ebk)

Printed in the United States of America

Contents

Introduction

I was in the sixth grade the first time I had trouble feeding myself. I had to rest my elbow on my control box, which allowed me to keep my arm in front of my mouth so I could put food in my mouth. I was able to pull my arm up and balance it on the box, not easy, but it worked. This was important to me because I had seen older kids with my disease being fed by someone else, and it freaked me out.

I am disabled. I have a muscle disease called "Duchenne Muscular Dystrophy." It deteriorates my muscles and their vitally important cells, slowly taking away the ability to take care of myself. I cannot feed myself, bathe myself, or clothe myself. In a nutshell, I have no physical independence. I rely completely on the help of other people, various kinds of technology, and many medications to live my life from day to day.

I have had to deal with many losses throughout my life. I had to let go of having a normal childhood and adolescence. Relationships with others have been, and are, difficult because I cannot participate in many social activities where I could build relationships. I cannot drive or go grocery shopping on my own. Spontaneous activities are trying because I need so much. Everything needs to be planned for.

I have been faced with death since the moment I was first diagnosed. That is very difficult even attempting to accept. The fact is that someday Duchenne Muscular Dystrophy will bring an end to my life. Instead of living in fear of that day, however, I have tried to embrace it. It is a fantastic opportunity to take stock of what is important and to live every moment completely, something many people never learn to do and end up on their deathbed finally seeing what they have missed.

There are many things life can teach us only through tragedy and loss. The biggest lesson we can learn through pain is that true independence is merely an illusion. Becoming dependent on something or someone is the only way to live a life of peace and fulfillment. Dependence is the purest form of humility, and humility is what gives meaning to our lives.

Facing this disability may sound bleak and depressing, as if I have no hope or reason to live. Truth be told, all of these terrible things have taught me lessons that most people will never have a chance to learn: Everyone needs to be dependent on others.

I know what you are thinking: "I'm not helpless, I can take care of myself. I'm completely independent." Perhaps your experiences so far in life have led you to that conclusion. The truth is that if you believe this, you are deluding yourself. John Donne was right when he said, "No man [or woman] is an island, entire of itself." We need one another. We are dependent upon one another.

Webster's dictionary defines being independent as "not requiring, or relying on, something else." Is that true for you? Do you not rely on anything or anyone else to live your life? The truth, dear human, is that your entire life is dependent on a myriad of variables. The entire universe is a set of systems that need one another in order to provide life. We cannot survive or sustain life independently. Here is a great example of the correct perspective we should all possess:

> President Theodore Roosevelt loved to spend his summers on San Juan Island, in the waters north of Seattle, near Victoria, British Columbia. If you've been there, you know what a beautiful spot it is. Roosevelt was a well-known lover of nature. One night, after an evening of conversation, he took a walk with his friend, William Beebe. They stopped and looked up at the vastness of the universe and were in awe of the Milky Way, the big and little dippers, and the endless black sky. Finally, Roosevelt broke the silence and said, "Now, I think we are small enough. Let's call it a night." [1]

Just as President Roosevelt did, we need to realize our position and status in the universe.

Dependence is a constant in every aspect of my physical life; I never had a choice in that. But you and I both have a greater choice. Being independent physically, as you see yourself, is not the end of the road. You are still limited in many things that you cannot do for yourself. The word "dependence" is not the best way to describe the position we are all in, even if you do not have to have someone else feed you. "Disability" is a much more powerful word picture. In most people's eyes the word "disabled" brings up an image of someone incapable of functioning like a "normal" person. I know the implication of this word. It means being weak, powerless, and helpless. Webster's dictionary defines disability as being "incapacitated by illness, injury, or wounds; *broadly*: physically or mentally impaired."

"Well," you might say, "doesn't that describe your position?" No. Because of my dependence (or disability) I have discovered what Blaise Pascal described as "a God-shaped vacuum in [my] life that only God can fill." So, looking at being disabled from a spiritual perspective, every one of us is incapacitated and impaired, unable to do anything that will be of eternal significance. My becoming "disabled" and so dependent on others to survive helped me discover, in 1994 "an inexpressible and glorious joy" as 1 Peter 1:8 puts it. I would like to explain to you what that Joy is.

1

Eating

As I said, I began to notice my ability to feed myself fading in sixth grade. I did not want to give up another ability and I had seen how older kids with MD looked while others fed them. One of these times was at an annual summer camp near Seattle that I attended for kids with Muscular Dystrophies of various kinds (there are forty different kinds of muscular dystrophy), many of them had Duchenne's just like me. Their ages varied from six to twenty-one and every person had different needs and abilities. It was a shock to see kids older then I who needed help to do *everything*. At every meal someone had to feed them by putting food to their mouths.

Some of these guys were on respirators, which really woke me up. They could not even breathe on their own, and I realized that this was my fate too. This camp was not all bad. I had some great experiences, which I will talk about later. It was also good be able to see that people could live despite having to be helped. Many of these people showed me that life was possible, even after Duchenne.

Around the beginning of my freshman year in high school my ability to feed myself dropped further. Two years prior, I had a surgery on my back to correct scoliosis. Now it had begun to affect my arm function. The next adaptation I made was to start using a hospital food tray that could be raised and lowered, and rolled around on wheels. I would have someone place my arms on top of the table next to my food. That way I was able to get food to my mouth, but it was still difficult. It worked for me, so I was satisfied. I could still avoid the thought of being fed by someone else.

At around age eighteen, I had to give up. I needed total help to eat anything. Now, whatever I eat, someone has to put it directly into my mouth! As reluctant as I was to see those days come, when my disease had progressed that far I was actually glad. I no longer had to struggle and keep adapting to stay ahead. I could relax and quit fighting, and it made my life easier. The truth is, when I finally gave up fighting, I gained so much more. I was now at peace because I finally had come to terms with my loss. I lost arm strength, but I gained mental and emotional strength.

If I had continued to fight the inevitable I would be deprived of the nutrition I needed to live well. I had to recognize that I was incapable of feeding myself. If I had not acknowledged that hard truth my hunger would never have been alleviated. Unless I acknowledged my inability, I would be in danger of losing the little I still had. I needed to ask for help or I would never get what I needed. Seeing my need for help allowed me to look beyond the problem and work on more important issues. It was taking so much effort to avoid and ignore the problems that, eventually, they would wear me down. Letting go allowed me to focus on the more important things in my life. This is still true as the disease progresses.

The same thing was true for my spirit. There were many things that I could not do spiritually without help. Ever since I was little I knew there was someone out there to help me, I just didn't recognize exactly who that was. Some major family issues led us to our first church, Capital Vision Christian Church, and Pastor Bruce Sanders. Pastor Bruce and some other great people at the church showed my family and me exactly where to look for help spiritually. No therapist, guru, author, or television celebrity could help. God alone can help us fulfill the needs of our spirit. When that special time came in 1994 when I found the inexpressible joy that I had been looking for, I was ready to acknowledge that there was an incredible experience awaiting me, if only I would quit fighting my dependence and yield to it. My newly born spirit needed to be fed, to be nourished and strengthened to enable spiritual growth. We can live for maybe a month without physical food. We can live much longer without spiritual food, but the results will be a hardened, empty life, one without hope. While all the time we think we are okay we are becoming spiritually bankrupt and very hungry.

Many of you do not see or believe that you need to be fed spiritually. "God is for the losers," you might say, or, "I don't need God. I can take care of myself ." You are being tricked by your own mind, your own worst enemy. You are spiritually dying because your pride will not admit that you need help. You will die without intervention from above. Let God feed you the sustenance and life you desperately need.

The Bible has a lot to say about our need for God to help us eat. I want to take some time and look at some specific verses that may help to illuminate what I am talking about.

He Who Comes to Jesus Will Never Go Hungry

Then Jesus declared, "I am the bread of life. He who comes to me will never go hungry" (John 6:35).

Jesus says here that in order to get this bread of life, which is eternal life, and keep from ever being hungry, we must come to Him. If I want to eat my dinner, I have to ask someone to help me or I won't eat. If I want to eat spiritual food, I must ask God to feed me. And, Jesus said, "The one who feeds on me will live because of me. This is the bread that came down from heaven" (vv. 57-58). No one else can give us the food that will fill that aching void in our spirits, or as Pascal said, that "God-shaped vacuum." Eternal food must be fed to us by the Eternal God.

How do we get God to feed us this eternal food? We simply need to surrender our own will and ask for His help. Then He will come to us and fill us up. We cannot feed ourselves the Bread of eternal life.

Not only do we need this Bread to become spiritually alive, we must continually feed on this Eternal Bread or our growth will be stunted. Sometimes Christians simply do not see their need to keep on letting God feed them; as a result their spirit just hangs on, near death, and they do not grow and mature. God wants us to rely completely on Him. If we try to feed ourselves and not humbly ask Him, out of a heart of hunger, to help us eat spiritual food, we will starve spiritually.

So many people rely on their own human efforts to get to the next level with God. They want and need to go beyond the "sin that so easily entangles" (Hebrews 12:1). But they hit the limits of how far they can go on their own and soon give up trying and just sit there, starving. The only way to truly know God more is to ask God to do what we cannot: Feed us the spiritual bread that will give us the strength needed to go beyond our limited human abilities.

The bottom line in this Scripture is in the most important words, "He who comes to me …" Where can you find the food that can never leave you hungry? It is only through the person of Jesus Christ that we can have our hunger met for eternity. You can search the entire world for something to fill the void. Many of us spend our energy attempting to find, in all the wrong places, the source of true peace, satisfaction, and fulfillment when the obvious thing to do is seek it at its source. If we use Jesus as our key, the door to peace and fulfillment will open.

Coming to Jesus, away from this world and our own way of living, is the only way to never be hungry again. Coming to Jesus is both the easiest and hardest thing we will ever have to do. It is hard because we have to give up every part of us to Him; it is easy because we can completely trust that our reward is far greater than any we would ever receive on our own. As He said, "Come to me and never go hungry" (see John 6:35).

We Must Eat of the Heavenly Bread

Our forefathers ate the manna in the desert; as it is written, "He gave them bread out of heaven to eat ..." I tell you the truth, it is not Moses who has given you the bread from heaven, but it is My Father who gives you the true bread from heaven (John 6:31-32).

After spending four hundred years in slavery, the Israelites who fled Egypt had to undergo tremendous hardship. They were utterly helpless to find food and water in the barren wilderness. They did not know how to hunt, and the "flocks and herds" they brought with them out of Egypt would not last long for six hundred thousand men, plus women and children. Especially since God began to require them to sacrifice their sheep, goats, and cattle to atone for their sins, which were many. They could not grow their food in the barren lands without adequate water. Nor did they spend enough time in one place for seed to sprout and bring fruition. They were disabled. Only when God stepped in could they be fed.

God did not choose to help the Israelites develop better hunting skills or give them a map to food and water. He met them at the place of their disability. Every night, for the next forty years, God dropped manna, food, from heaven. He simply told them to go out each morning and collect enough food for only one day's supply. Then the people began to complain that they were sick of manna: "The Israelites started wailing and said, 'If only we had meat to eat! We remember the fish we ate in Egypt at no cost—also the cucumbers, melon, leeks, onions and garlic. But now we have lost our appetite; we never see anything but this manna!'" (Numbers 11:4-6). One night a strong wind "from the Lord" drove quail in from the sea and dropped them all around the camp.

It took awhile before the Israelites realized that they could not do for themselves; they had to lose their independence and humbly look to God for life.

Several hundred years later, by the time Jesus appeared, the people once again had to be shown that they were truly unable to help themselves. The religious Jews in first-century Palestine had become proud, indignant, and self-righteous. They tried to outdo one another in looking to their religious works to save themselves—not only by obeying the Laws of Moses, but even more laws that they had made up. In their minds the laws had become their ticket to salvation. However, the Bible says in, Romans 3:20: "Therefore no one will be declared righteous in his [God's] sight by observing the law." They still needed God to step in and feed them because they could not feed themselves.

Once again the Bread came from heaven. This time the allotment was not for one day at a time for only forty years. This time the bread would last for eternity. These "righteous" Jews, on their own, could do nothing to become righteous in God's eyes, and neither can we. We must recognize that we are disabled spiritually and need to call on God to give us the "Bread from heaven" if we are to become righteous: "God made him who had no sin to be sin for us, so that in him we might become the righteousness of God" (2 Corinthians 5:21).

In the wilderness the Israelites looked to Moses for their salvation. They did not complain to God, they complained to Moses. They blamed Moses for making them leave Egypt and their "good life" and bringing them into a desert where they would surely die. Fortunately, Moses was "a very humble man, more humble than anyone else on the face of the earth" (Numbers 12:3), and he knew that salvation would come only from God.

That is what Jesus was trying to teach the religious Jews. "He who comes to me will never go hungry" (John 6:35). We can do nothing to save ourselves, nor can we do anything to grow and mature on our own. When we allow God complete reign to feed us one day at a time, real growth can occur. We have to let our pride fall away, and humbly allow our Father to feed us what we need if we are to survive spiritually. Just as the Jews did, we try to use religion as a way to feed ourselves, but there is no other way than through Christ Jesus. No amount of prayer, worship, or Bible study can feed us this eternal life; only the hand of God. Just as the manna in the wilderness could not be duplicated by human effort, neither can salvation be found through human effort, "For there is no other name under heaven given to men by which we must be saved" (Acts 4:12). God alone could produce the lifeline that the Israelites desperately needed. The same goes for so many who are wandering through the wilderness of this life.

Whoever Eats of the Bread of Heaven Will Live Forever

Then Jesus declared, "I am the bread of life. He who comes to me will never go hungry, and he who believes in me will never be thirsty.... I am the living bread that came down from heaven. If a man eats of this bread, he will live forever. This bread is my flesh, which I will give for the life of the world" (John 6:35, 51).

The Israelites got only one day's supply of bread at once. If they tried to save any of it until the next day it became "full of maggots and began to smell" (Exodus 16:20). The bread of heaven is the only food we can eat that will never rot and begin to smell. This bread is the key to life for every person on earth. We eat natural food so that our bodies will not grow weak, cease to function, and then die. The bread of heaven is different because it feeds and maintains our spirit.

Jesus said that just as the Israelites ate manna, bread, from heaven in order to live, we also must eat the bread "that comes down from heaven" so that we might live. Jesus, of course, is speaking metaphorically. He did not expect the disciples to literally eat His flesh. He is saying that we have to accept this Manna from heaven every day as if it were food so that we will be nourished and live for all eternity. If we partake of this bread of heaven we cannot die. Our bodies will die because they are flesh, but our spirits will live forever in the presence of the Eternal God. In order to strengthen and enable our spirits to live to their potential, we need the things of the spirit. Without partaking of this Bread we will be weak and unable to accomplish anything God asks us to do.

Jesus tells His listeners that "if a man eats of this bread" (v. 51) he will live forever. The Bread is available, but we must accept it. God will never force-feed us no matter how obvious our need, how spiritually starved we are. God is patiently waiting for us. Hoping we will come and say, "Lord, give me the bread of heaven so my spirit can live forever." Just as the religious Jews did in Jesus day—faithfully living by every word of Moses' Laws and the ones they made up—we try to gain eternal life by working at it, living independently of Jesus. We reject the truth that Jesus alone is the bread of heaven. We must stop living in independence; away from the Source of our eternal, spiritual, bread. There is no other way to grow spiritually except to ask for and eat the Bread of heaven. Jesus makes it plain enough in Matthew 7:7-8, "Ask, and it will be given to you; seek, and you will find; knock, and the door will be opened to you. For everyone who asks receives, and he who seeks finds, and to him who knocks, the door will be opened."

Many of you reading this book have tried everything to find a deeper meaning to life. You have looked everywhere for something to satisfy that aching need for fulfillment. You have done many things that you hope will have eternal significance. Here is a great picture of what this looks like:

> Let's evaluate this. You can't control your moods. A few of your relationships are shaky. You have fears and faults. Hmmm. Do you really want to hang on to your chest of self-reliance? Sounds to me as if you could use a shepherd. Otherwise, you might end up with a Twenty-third Psalm like this: I am my own shepherd. I am always in need. I stumble from mall to mall and shrink to shrink, seeking relief but never finding it. I creep through the valley of the shadow of death and fall apart. I fear everything from pesticides to power lines, and I'm starting to act like my mother. I go down to the weekly staff

> meeting and am surrounded by enemies. I go home, and even my goldfish scowls at me. I anoint my headache with extra-strength Tylenol. My Jack Daniel's runneth over. Surely misery and misfortune will follow me, and I will live in self-doubt for the rest of my lonely life. [2]

If you desperately are looking for something to fill the vacuum in your life, that deep emptiness in your soul, here is some advice. Quit being stubborn by trying to feed yourself. Give up and reach out to the source of spiritual strength. Receive the bread of heaven given to us through the sacrifice of Christ. Ask for this bread and you will receive it. You will go deeper than humanly possible, tapping into the power of eternity. You will never die; your eternal future can be laid out in front of you. Run to Jesus immediately, ask Him for the bread of heaven. For some reason we are cursed with a desire to be rebellious. We are always attempting to gain heaven by doing it ourselves. If you have been running away in rebellion, I know you are tired and weak. I know you need peace and rest. Simply turn around and run to Jesus so He can change your tired and weary life. In return, He will feed you the bread of heaven and give you a new life designed for eternity in heaven. Run to Jesus, and live forever.

We Must Partake of This Bread Every Day

Give us each day our daily bread (Luke 11:3).

This verse comes from the passage where the disciples asked Jesus to teach them how they are meant to pray. Jesus gives them this example of prayer, more commonly known as the Lord's Prayer. It is apparent that Jesus believed this bread was very important. Important enough that we should pray to receive it on a daily basis. The bread is important because it gives our spirit the strength it needs to live within God's will every day. It is easy to attain, but hard to find because God alone holds an eternal supply of it.

While Jesus lived with His disciples He fed them every day. Now that Christ is in His rightful place at the right hand of God, we need a way to be fed. Prayer, or asking for God's help, is the only way to find what we are after. God alone can give us this bread you need.

The hardest thing to give up is our own will, our own independence. We must acknowledge that we are disabled, and we do this only by coming to God in our weakness and accepting the power that we have been promised. Asking Him to feed us and allowing Him to be our provider is the only hope we have to gain the power available in the bread. When we eat in the physical world, we do it to survive. Having God feed you spiritually will allow you to do more than just survive.

The spiritual bread God will feed you gives you a power beyond your own human limitations. If you do not come to God and ask him for help, your spirit will waste away. Even more, you will live a life without the power to change yourself or others.

Why is it so hard to accept the truth that we need help if we are to be spiritually fed every day of our lives on this earth? I believe the reason is that raw, unchecked pride gets in our way at every turn. Pride says, "I am living fine on my own today, I don't need to eat. Besides, I ate what I needed last Sunday at church." This pride that lives within us all is powerful and deadly to our spirit. Satan had that same pride before he fell. Isaiah tells us that he said in his heart, "I will ascend to heaven; I will raise my throne above the stars of God" (14:13). He believed God was no longer needed for him to be satisfied. Very quickly, he reaped the consequences, and will for all eternity. In the same way, when you allow pride to speak for you, your spirit will suffer. It will starve, lose its power, separate from God, and rot away.

Remove all pride and your spirit will regain its strength, reconnect with God, and come back to life. Not only will your spirit live, it will be vibrant, strong, and powerful. The bread must be eaten daily to keep your life flourishing, able to change the world with the power of God. It will take a lot of humility to admit that you cannot help yourself to it and to ask God for it. Despite that, remember that weakness allows us to receive everything we need to be strong.

2

Drinking

The first time I was unable to pick up a cup and get it to my mouth was frustrating. I knew that this meant I could never drink anything by myself. One more ability was taken away.

Many times I felt as if I would be unable to cope. Yet, times like these can be the most important moments a person can face. In moments like these you come face to face with reality. I knew that many other normal actions would be taken away, and there was absolutely nothing I could do to stop it. This was the moment of decision. I could either go down the path of denial and feel sorry for myself, or realize the reality of the situation and not allow it to hold me back. I decided to accept another disability and yield to whatever would happen. If I was going to need help to drink, that was okay.

When I was in middle school and the muscles in my arms began to fail me I began to improvise. I would swing my arm up in such a way that my elbow would land on my driving control box. That way I could pick up a cup and get it to my mouth. But if I had something else in my hand, the task became more difficult. However, I was bound and determined to continue drinking on my own.

Before long I needed to have someone place a cup or drink box in my hand once I had balanced my arm. Looking back, these little bumps seem so small, but at the time they were mountains to climb. Day after day my weakness became more apparent, and I was forced to become more humbled.

About midway through high school I could no longer balance my arms. I had to rest them on a hospital tray to hold up a drink—if someone was there to place the drink in my hand. I desperately hung on to one of the last bits of independence. Soon, however, all of this improvisation became too much for me. I now faced the final fork in the road as far as drinking was concerned. I had to let go of another ability. I could no longer help myself. The only control left to me was how I would cope with the facts. I decided to remain positive and not allow the negative facts to affect my life. The truth is, that just like my eating, it became much easier to simply let others help me to drink. While this was difficult for me, the end result was far less stressful. Yet again, giving up actually gave me peace and changed my attitude. I finally got a bunch of straws from Costco. Costco, naturally, had giant bags of about 3,000 straws. I would have someone fill up a mug, put a straw in it, and place it either on my tray or the kitchen counter so I could get to it.

The hardest part was conquering my pride and giving up more of my own ability. "Why was that so important?" you might be asking. Well, I'll tell you why. A human can live without water for only a very short time. The most we can expect to live without water is eight to ten days. Water is what our life depends on. In fact, all life is completely dependent upon it. Water is so important that 75 percent of our earth is covered by it. Food gives us strength. Water gives us life. A lack of food will leave us weak and without energy. Going a short period of time without water will kill us.

Water is also valuable because it creates energy through dams that power very large areas. Without water, most of the United States would be shut down and blacked out. But water can also be very dangerous if it is mistreated. Clean water gives us life; polluted water can be deadly. Water is necessary for all physical life. Water is just as important and powerful in the spiritual life.

Spiritual water, or what the Bible calls "living water," is similar to natural water in some ways. but it is also very different. Spiritual water gives life to our spirit. We must maintain a healthy level in order to allow our spirit to live the way it was meant to. Without spiritual water our spirit will wilt away and die in the same way our body would. We must continue to refill our spirit with water to stay healthy. This is one of the similarities between natural water and spiritual water, but the differences are where things get interesting.

Spiritual water is alive. It helps connect us to God. I like to think of it as our spiritual umbilical cord. When Jesus met the woman at the Jacob's well He asked her for a drink. Then He told her, "If you knew the gift of God and who it is that asks you for a drink, you would have asked him and he would have given you living water" (John 4:10). Then He said, "Whoever drinks the water that I give him will never thirst. Indeed, the water I give him will become in him a spring of water welling up to eternal life" (v. 14). When we drink this live water, God is allowed to move in our lives in a way not otherwise possible. The great thing is that this is not a one-time event. If we are filled with living water we are connected to God for eternity. What a great idea! If we simply maintain a healthy level of spiritual water, God is able to do amazing things in our lives. He is able to speak amazing things into our lives. He is also able to lead us to do amazing things with our own lives.

Natural water is found in various places throughout the world. There are more sources and ways to get water than I can describe. Drinking water can come from a glacier, rain, evaporation, chemical reactions, and even from salt water. The water of the spirit is very different. It only comes from one place: God Himself. And there is only one way to get it: ask for it. You cannot find it anywhere else, only by asking God for it.

This all sounds very narrow minded, but there is a good reason why you can only get it from one Source. We cannot dig it from the earth, dip it from a well, capture it from a spring, or catch it from the clouds. We are not big enough, clever enough, or self-sufficient enough to get it for ourselves. It must come from God, the source of everything we need. Most of us know that, given the choice, we will ignore God. But ignoring Him will only bring our destruction. God knows about our disability to save ourselves, so He alone can save us. What a great way to get our attention! Drinking the Living Water helps to keep us committed. We have to stay committed in order to reap the benefits of spiritual water. We cannot just fill up once and go on with our lives. The water we take in is constantly being poured out. We are in constant need of a refill and renewal. Drinking the Living Water makes us humble. Humility enables our spirits to change. God is looking to get these three things from us: attention, commitment, and humility.

Those who refuse to recognize this fact will remain spiritually dead, unable to grow. They try to keep their spirit alive through their own efforts. They fill their spirit up with sex, drugs, relationships, false religions, spiritualities, and philosophies. All of these things will give our spirits life for only a short time. After this short time, more is needed to keep us going. Once the pleasure of these things fades away, only emptiness remains. Then we have to resort to something else and the cycle continues.

God alone, through Christ, can give us life through a three-part process. First, we must let go of our own ability to drink and *come to God for help*. Second, we must *ask God to help us drink*. Lastly, we must *allow God to help us*. He will not help us unless we are fully committed to His help. Spiritual water is the only way to let your spirit live to its potential. Only through living water can we be connected to God and be able to do more than we can imagine.

Come to God for Help

Jesus stood and said in a loud voice, "If a man is thirsty, let him come to me and drink. Whoever believes in me, as the scripture has said, streams of living water will flow from within him." By this he meant the Spirit, whom those who believed in him were later to receive (John 7:37-38).

Way back in Jeremiah 2:13, God said, "My people have committed two sins: they have forsaken me, the spring of living water, and have dug their own cisterns, broken cisterns that cannot hold water." God is saying in a very powerful way that we absolutely need Him. The Jews that Jeremiah was preaching to had lost their connection to God. They decided to go their own way and do things on their own. As a result, they failed miserably and ended up in the hands of their enemies. Going our own way will produce the same results. We will fail and be pushed around by every plot of our enemy.

This verse is interesting because of the imagery that Jeremiah uses. A cistern is an artificial water reservoir. They would basically dig out a giant hole and let the water fill up the hole. It was an easy way to get the water they so dearly needed. If the cistern failed than the entire community was without water. It had to be made exact or risk a horrible disaster.

God was telling the Jews in the days of Jeremiah, and is telling the people of today, that attempting to build a faulty cistern will end badly. God is saying that the only way to build the cistern correctly is to rely on Him to build it. Instead of going our own way and trying to build our own cisterns that will break, we must come to Him. Ignoring God is only going to lead to faulty construction. When times get tough don't be the one that falls apart because you did not build your cistern exactly the way it was supposed to be made.

Ask God for Help

Jesus answered her, "If you knew the gift of God and who it is that asks you for a drink, you would have asked him and he would have given you living water" (John 4:10).

We can see here that if we are to get water, God himself must give it to us. Jesus told this woman, who happened to be a Samaritan, that she had to ask for it to get it.

There is a lot of significance in the fact that this woman was a Samaritan. First, being a woman made her less than a man in this culture. Second, being a Samaritan meant that Jews would look down upon her even more because the Jews considered them as half-castes. Why are these significant issues? I think it is significant because God is not class conscious, anybody can access living water. Despite the fact that many of us may be looked down upon by others in some way, we can have access to the same things as everybody else.

I believe that another major part of this verse is the beginning, "If you knew the gift of God …" This shows where many of us are unable to see God's gift because of our pride. The woman was so intent on getting water herself, she did not see the preciousness of the gift that was before her. Yes, she was there to draw physical water herself, but Jesus spoke of living water, or spiritual water. Living water is the spiritual force that gives life to our spirit. Without it our spirit will die. For this woman, as it is for many people, it was difficult for her to recognize her need for living water. She had Jesus Himself, the Living Water, before her and she could not recognize it. We are no different. God and His water are before us.

Before we are able to ask for this spiritual, living water, which we need, we must recognize that it is critical to our spirits. That is the whole point of this book. I want you, if you are a believer, to recognize that you need help to live a victorious, fruitful, totally satisfying life in Christ. We are disabled, and we must see the gifts that will come to us when we recognize that we are disabled. Once we recognize our needs and that these incredible gifts are available to us I believe we will do whatever we have to do to get them, even humbling ourselves. Jesus was saying here that until we recognize our total dependence on Him, we probably will not ask for His help. He wanted the woman to come to Him for this water. She needed to allow God to give her the water that only He could bring her.

Later in this story we find that this woman thought that relationships would keep her going, but these attempts had failed. She had been married five times and currently was in another relationship. I think Jesus gave her this opportunity so that she would recognize her need for help. Her spirit was dying and longing for the life that only the Messiah, this man standing before her, could give her. God wants to give each and every one of us the same opportunity. This verse teaches us that God wants to give us a great gift. No matter who you are, you can receive it.

God is standing before you at the well. He desires more than anything for you to recognize Him and the gift He has to give you. God wants to give you the gift, but you must allow Him to do so. He will not force it upon you. You must want it because you need it and must ask for it before you can receive it. God's gifts can all be summed up this way. Any gift that God gives us will last forever and be exactly what we need to do His will.

Accept God's Help

The woman said to him, "Sir, give me this water" (John 4:15).

In the book of Acts we find Paul and Silas in a prison in Philippi because they were preaching about Jesus. "About midnight Paul and Silas were praying and singing hymns to God … Suddenly there was such a violent earthquake that … the prison doors flew open, and everybody's chains came loose." When the jailer woke up and realized that all the doors were open he drew his sword to kill himself. Paul called out to him that everybody was still there. The jailer was so impressed that he asked, "Men, what must I do to be saved?" He asked Paul and Silas to give him the living water. (See Acts 16:25-30.) Paul explained that he must believe in the Lord Jesus and he would be saved.

That was the beginning of the jailer's spiritual life, but he would need to drink of this living water regularly. Jesus explained this when He was talking to the Samaritan woman. "Everyone who drinks this water will be thirsty again; but whoever drinks the water that I give him will never thirst. Indeed, the water that I give him will become in him a spring of water welling up to eternal life" (John 4:13-14). Jesus said that when we receive this water we do not get it just once. Rather, it will be like a spring that continues to quench our thirst forever.

Jesus tells the woman at the well the difference between natural water and the spiritual water He can give. Drinking natural water from a well satisfies only temporarily; she will get thirsty again. This describes the result of our own efforts to fuel our spirit. There are many things in this world that can give us a temporary spiritual high and quench our thirsts for a short while. The kicker is that our spirit's needs must be fulfilled constantly and continually.

No worldly thing that we try to fill our spirit with will satisfy for long. We will always need more. Our spirit is from God and can never be satisfied by this world. Sex, drugs, relationships, idols of various kinds, religion, music, money, fame, power and all other worldly substitutes will never satisfy us. These things will only last for a time and you will soon have to get a new fix. So you go to something else. This leads us to addiction and many other ugly things. Spiritual, living water is the only thing that will fill our spirit up completely and eternally. We will always have access to it. It is the only thing that can fill your spirit without leading to destruction. We will never be empty, and the stress of constantly refilling will give way to true peace. The peace comes from knowing that we do not have to constantly find new ways to satisfy our spirit. What a great gift that God wants to give to us! Satisfaction will no longer be an issue. We can have a complete feeling of contentment.

God has a great desire to see our lives changed, complete and full of abundance. John 10:10 says, "I came that they may have life, and have it abundantly." This verse is what God is all about. He not only wants to save our souls, He wants to give us everything we need. This is true when God helps us drink living water. He not only wants to provide life to our spirit. He wants us to have life forever. We do not have to be barely alive, in a state of survival, only taking enough water to care for ourselves. Instead, we can have an abundant life, so much life that we can give it away. Spiritual water can help us to live that life. We will have the potential and ability to carry out whatever God asks us to do.

This is where many Christians get stuck. They believe in God and want to follow Him but recognize that something is missing; they do not feel fulfilled and find that their faith wavers. They need the water that only God can give them. Without it they are empty and without power. I think of it as a fire hydrant with no water. When the firefighters come and need to utilize the hydrant they have no water to put out the fire. The firefighters are unable to do their job effectively and people may die because of it. We need to be full of water in order to do our jobs. If we cannot do our job effectively people may die spiritually and never find a satisfying eternity.

Jesus finishes this verse with the final promise that His water will become an eternal, overflowing well of life within us. This well is always nearby and easily accessed when we are in need of fulfillment. No matter what trials and tribulations we face, the living water is within reach and can give instant relief. This is the true purpose for letting God help us to drink. When we humbly allow God to help us He will place a well in our hearts. Once He does, we can drink from it. The great thing is, this well never runs dry, it is always overflowing. It is easily found because it is always available, not just for us, but for every person around us.

The water that overflows is more than enough to give people a taste. But just a taste, an emotional high, a brief glimpse into heaven is not enough. Many people have drunk living water from God's cup, but not all of them have asked for the overflowing well to be placed within their hearts.

My only source of strength is that overflowing well. If God had not put the well of living water within my heart, I would have no hope. People sometimes wonder where my strength and perseverance come from; they come from the well. The living water overflows from the well and covers everything around me, giving me strength and perseverance. God is giving you a chance to have that strength too. That eternal, overflowing well of living water is available to you. Come to Him and allow Him to help you to take the first drink and then allow

Him to place that well within your heart. Trust me, if you do your life will change forever.

This idea of water from a well that always overflows is not just in the New Testament. In Exodus we read that when the Israelites escaped from Egypt and Pharaoh and were wandering in the desert of Sinai, after a while without the rich Nile River at their front doors they began to be in need of water. They complained heavily to Moses that they needed a drink to satisfy their thirst. They blamed Moses, but Moses knew that God could be relied upon to supply their need. God told Moses, "I will stand before you by the rock at Horeb. Strike the rock, and water will come out of it for the people to drink" (Exodus 17:6).

The people needed water and God provided it. As ridiculous as it seems, God told Moses to take his staff and hit a rock, breaking it and sending water gushing from it. Moses never asked why, he simply obeyed and all the people had their thirst satisfied. Once again, God proved that He would provide for His children when they asked.

This passage also has great significance for every one of us today. Many times I feel as if I cannot continue. I feel like my hope is gone, that my life has no meaning. I know that is something we can all relate to. Those are the times when I need God to satisfy my thirst. When I have been spiritually wandering and I have to be filled up again, I simply ask God, and He provides the water I need. We do not need to force God to give us this water, we just need to ask for it. Moses found this out at the waters of Meribah. Once again the people complained about not having any water. God told Moses to take his staff and, with his brother Aaron, go to a rock and speak to it and it would bring forth water. Moses had probably had enough of these people. Instead of speaking to the rock, asking for water, he pounded on it twice. Yes, water gushed out and everybody had water. But his disobedience had repercussions. After leading these stubborn people for forty years, Moses would not have the privilege of entering the Promised Land. (See Numbers 20:6-13.)

No matter what situation we face or what condition our spirit is in, there is a rock to strike to give us life. Remember that Jesus is our source of living water. He is the rock that is always there in our time of need. It is up to us to come forward in faith and humility and strike the rock. The water we need is always available but we must actively seek it. The rock might be a great thing to find, but that is not enough. In his song just before he died, Moses sang about the Rock, whose works are perfect, and whose ways are just (see Deuteronomy 32).

God Wants You to Have This Water

So now I have a few questions for you. First, will you recognize your thirst? Second, will you seek the Rock, the source of the water you need? And third, will you passionately, ardently, do whatever it takes to get to the water? If you do these three things you can be filled with spiritual life no matter what trouble you face. God is looking for people who will desperately seek Him and His gifts. God is hidden from us so that we will take the effort to find Him. When God knows that we are actively, sincerely looking for the gifts He has waiting, He will give them to us because our motives are right. Let God fill you up in every situation you encounter, whether good or bad. In the end, you will have the strength and hope it takes to continue.

In Paul's letter to the Corinthians he referred to this time in the desert when God's people needed water. "And by a miracle God sent them food to eat and water to drink there in the desert; they drank the water that Christ gave them. He was there with them as a mighty Rock of spiritual refreshment" (1 Corinthians 10:3-4, *TLB*). Paul wrote this to the Corinthians to show them that God could help them in the same way he helped the Israelites in the wilderness. God wants to help you too, today. Christ was with the Israelites and provided for their great need. If you choose to come to Him with your need He will miraculously feed you and satisfy your thirst.

God's greatest desire is to be our provider. He is simply waiting for you to give Him an opportunity. Someone once put it to me this way. "God is always walking behind us no matter where we go. Even when we are running away, He is right behind us. The quickest path to God's help is to turn around and meet Him face to face." God is nearer and easier to reach than you know. Turn to Him and let Him have the opportunity to satisfy your thirst.

The only person that could provide for the Israelites in their time of need was God. During the forty years of wandering the Israelites endured, this was very obvious. Without God they had no hope. There was no way to avoid that fact. But once the Israelites reached their promised land they began to backslide from God. What happened that caused this change? God never moved away from them. The Israelites moved away from God because they stopped letting Him be their sole provider.

We have the same problem as the Israelites. Often we tend to back away from God. Why? The level of our dependence is the level of our spiritual effectiveness. The less we rely on God, the less we can do spiritually. That equation must be balanced properly or we cannot feel peace. Make an effort today and everyday to keep that equation balanced. Godly Dependence = Spiritual Effect. This is one of the great principles that God has placed within His kingdom. We are only as effective as God makes us. God is keenly aware of this principle within our lives. He will not give us tasks that we are unable to carry out. The more effective we are, the more we can accomplish.

We must be filled spiritually with the living water that only God can give us. This is not something that we can do on our own. We must ask God to help us drink this living water. We must actively search out the hidden sources that God has made. It is placed within us but must be searched for in order to test our motives. God wants us to come before Him, recognizing our needs, and allowing Him to make us spiritually effective. We need spiritual, living water if we are to have any sort of connection with God. This connection is what gives us the strength to carry out God's will. Don't waste any more time. Take the example of the Samaritan woman at the well. Recognize that Jesus is before you with the gift of living water and ask him for it. Once you do, your life will never be the same.

3

Washing

As it is with any activity in my life, I need a lot of help to do what it takes to keep my body clean. In fact I need complete help to wash myself and maintain good hygiene. Reaching this point of complete dependence, like all other self-care, was a gradual process. For a few years I was able to brush my teeth and take baths on my own. Then I slowly started to lose the ability to do even the most basic of hygiene tasks. I could not wash my hands. I could not comb my hair. I would never be able to shave.

Brushing my teeth was possible for awhile because I would rest my arms on my trusty hospital tray, then brush my teeth. I was unable to reach the sink, so I would have to rinse out my mouth by spitting into a bowl. Soon, lack of arm strength forced me to start using an electric toothbrush. As my strength waned more and more I had to relent and allow others to take control and brush my teeth.

This gradual erosion of independence was one of the most difficult to go through. I felt that I was losing all dignity. I had to give up all my control over my own hygiene. I had no choice but to let others help me. However, I did have a choice in how I dealt with it. I could choose to rebel or resent those who would help me. But I chose to take it as it came and deal with it as best I could.

Despite this decision, I soon realized that more challenges and adaptations would need to be met. I needed to keep my body clean, for obvious reasons. First I started using a bath seat to keep me from falling in the shower. Someone would seat me on the seat and I would then wash myself. I still use the shower seat, but now someone else does all of the washing for me.

This was one of the hardest things for me, allowing somebody to wash me. It was a real struggle to become humble enough to do that. Understandably, giving up control of such a personal area of my life was a gut check. Swallowing my pride here meant facing a whole new level of humiliation. I have to let someone see me naked and to take complete care of me. This is something I still have to deal with over and over again. With every new caregiver I get, I face the same battle. Many of you surely take this for granted and probably never think about it. That's why I want to talk about it. Maybe you will learn not to take things for granted and, rather than feeling as if you are losing your independence, be grateful that help is available.

A lot of people on the street do without brushing their teeth or cleaning their bodies. Right? A lot of those people also have a great number of problems. There are two reasons why it is important to wash and maintain a state of cleanliness. The first reason is concrete and tangible. We need to wash to rid ourselves of harmful bacteria and fungus that live in our skin. If we do not wash away the bad things clinging to our bodies we will face health problems that can affect our lives in major ways and prevent us from living the way we want to.

For many centuries, we were unaware of the existence and power of germs. This discovery changed the world dramatically. We now know that if germs are not washed away they will be passed on to other people, making them ill or even killing them. Up until the late 1800s doctors did not understand why many of their patients became sick or even died after surgeries. Later, the reason for these illnesses and deaths became clear. Doctors were not washing away the germs from themselves and were passing them on during their treating procedures. Once we realized that the germs were the cause, we found ways to cleanse ourselves of them, which completely changed our state of health.

The other reason we need to wash ourselves has more to do with our culture than anything else. We want to present ourselves to other members of society in an acceptable way. Today's culture puts a high value on cleanliness. We judge each other on how we look (and how we smell). We judge each other on how well we take care of ourselves. It is a rather shallow way of looking at things. We are very interested in outward appearance. Like it or not, it is a very important aspect of our lives. Being dirty and not hygienic is looked down upon. As a result, we are very concerned with how others perceive us. We want to present ourselves in an acceptable way to those who will judge us. Without washing ourselves and maintaining cleanliness we will be judged negatively.

Where did all of this leave me? I felt that yet again I had to get over my inability to help myself and the pride involved with not wanting help. I had no choice in the matter. The voice in my mind might have been against that, but the disease had a louder voice. While this whole process has been quite difficult and humbling, the alternative is not an option. I cannot live my life without bathing and washing. My life would have less quality if I were dirty. I would have a multitude of health issues and nobody could bear the smell. I would not be able to present myself the way I would like. I had to give in and allow help or I would not have much of a life.

Our spiritual lives are no different. Our spirit needs to be clean through washing. Same as our bodies, there are why this is important. First, our spiritual health is at stake. The germs, bacteria, and fungus must be washed away or they will cause problems that can lead to sickness and death. If we avoid cleansing ourselves of these things through either ignorance or denial we not only endanger ourselves spiritually, but all of those we come in contact with. Second, we can infect large groups of people without even knowing it. I want to give you the knowledge of the germs we all carry. Just as our physical knowledge of germs changed our state of health as a culture, spiritual knowledge can change our spiritual state of health. Not just for ourselves, but all those we come in contact with.

Sin Is a Powerful Infection

Sin is a disgrace to any people (Proverbs 14:34).

Everyone, as a product of being human, carries with them a kind of bacteria. It is a fungus that grows at a tremendous rate. It is a powerful germ that can be carried along to anyone, anywhere, and anytime. Spiritually speaking, we call this junk, sin. Left unchecked and unwashed it is a powerful infection. Sin is the worst kind of filth. It covers every inch of our spirit like mud. Sin leads our spirit towards all sorts of illness and, as Romans 6:23 says, that sin leads toward death. Having the knowledge of sin is important, but what you do about it is of greater magnitude. Many people have different views of exactly what sin is all about. However, it would be safe to say that, in essence, sin is anything we do that separates us from God.

This separation from God has deep consequences. Since Adam and Eve succumbed to their first encounter with sin we have lived a harsh, painful, temporary existence on earth. We wake every morning knowing that we may suffer pain, disappointment, and emptiness. All positive elements of life could one day be gone for eternity. It is an ugly subject, but sin has a profound effect on all of our lives.

Not only does sin contaminate our day-to-day existence, a more grave consequence of sin lies ahead. When our life here on earth ends, the effect of sin will still remain upon us. Like filth on our unwashed bodies, if we are not properly cleansed from sin, what we experience on earth will continue forever. We will have pain and suffering for as long as time. Most importantly, this separation from God means that we can never connect with Him and never live out His will for us. Our purpose here is to glorify God and have a relationship with Him. Sin is a kind of barricade that keeps us from what we were meant for. If we are covered in sin, God is repelled. He cannot dwell where there is sin.

What can we do to solve the problems that sin can cause? Well, just as we wash away the dirt and other harmful elements from our body, we must wash away sin. However, just as I have to submit to someone else to wash my body, we cannot possibly cleanse ourselves from the consequences of sin. This is where we need God's help. Try as we might, and we all have, our own efforts to wash away our sin are futile. Until you are clean He cannot take you to the next level in your spirit.

Recognize Your Need for Cleansing

Wash away all my iniquity and cleanse me from my sin (Psalm 51:2).

These are the words David, the most notable king of Israel, prayed when he wrote this particular psalm. Most of us know David as the teenager that killed Goliath with his slingshot and a smooth stone. He is remembered as a good king and an even greater man. First Samuel 13:14 calls him, a man after God's own heart. Obviously, his reputation is very powerful. He was a man full of character and righteousness. But David had a problem; he was a man. This was a problem because, like all of us, David was covered in sin. As great a man as he was, sometimes he needed that sin washed from him.

David wrote this psalm after Nathan, a prophet and great, close friend, confronted him. Nathan uncovered David's infamous attempt to cover sins involving a woman named Bathsheba, and Uriah, her husband and devoted soldier. Second Samuel 11 tells us the story. As was customary, most kings went out to fight their wars at springtime. David ordered Israel to attack and destroy the Ammonites, laying siege to a city called Rabbah. For whatever reason, King David decided to stay home instead of going to war. In his place, he sent General Joab.

In my mind his reason for staying becomes pretty obvious. Perhaps he had previously seen his neighbor Bathsheba, whom Samuel describes as being very beautiful, bathing on her rooftop, as was the custom. One night, after his soldiers went off to war, he went up to the roof of his palace and looked over at his neighbor's house and saw Bathsheba. Perhaps Bathsheba was aware that she was being observed. Her husband was away, fighting, a great deal of the time, and she was lonely. It is hard to believe that David accidentally witnessed this event. I believe that this was his intent for staying home. I think this fact is important because it shows that David sinned as easily and as big as we do. It also shows how deep into it he had fallen.

After he watched her for some time, he had her brought to the palace. Later, David sleeps with her, falling even deeper by committing adultery. He sends her away having his lust satisfied, believing that to be the end of it. Well, as we know, sex, as well as sin, has strong consequences. Sure enough, the conspiracy escalates when David learns that Bathsheba is pregnant. Rather than face and deal with these consequences, David resorts to a cover up. It was a conspiracy that could make Watergate look like Babygate.

David sent for Bathsheba's husband Uriah to come home from the front lines of the battle. David was hoping Uriah would return and sleep with his wife. David needed the timing of the pregnancy not to raise suspicion or reveal the truth. Things did not go as planned. Uriah was more loyal to his fellow soldiers than David bargained for. Uriah refused Bathsheba because he could not justify his pleasure in the face of his comrades' struggles. So, David chose to sin further by continuing his cover up. He ordered Joab to put Uriah on the front lines of the enemy's strongest position. David's sinful conspiracy was complete when Uriah died on the battlefield. After Bathsheba went through a time of grieving, David made her his wife and she soon birthed his child.

I believe God waited nine months to give David an opportunity to ask for forgiveness of his sin, to be washed clean. David figured he could get out of this dilemma his own way, which meant Uriah had to die some time within the nine months of Bathsheba's pregnancy. David did not accept God's plan to repent to God, instead he tried to wash himself clean. God decided to get David's attention. After the child was born the Lord sent Nathan to David. God used Nathan to prick David's heart, making him realize that his attempts to wash himself had failed. God wanted David to see that only God could wash away and cleanse him from sin. Nathan tells a story of a rich man that owns many sheep but chooses to take the only lamb that a poor man owns. The rich man uses the poor man's lamb to feed a guest, instead of killing his own. David became furious with the sin of the rich man, not knowing the story was about him.

When Nathan revealed the true nature of the tale, David finally admitted his guilt and became honest about the depth of his sin. David repented and gave his sin to God at that moment and asked God to cleanse him. Then, and only then, was David truly cleansed of his sin. At that moment David understood exactly what he needed and became very aware of his dependence on God through this experience. Then he wrote the psalm.

I believe that this moment in history means a lot to us today. Every one of us has committed sin and separated ourselves from God, but it is what we do about it that counts. God wanted David to repent of his adultery so that He could wash it away, but David tried to wash himself. However, he continued in his sin and paid the price: he lost his baby son.

Let us not make the same mistake. Do not let sin get out of hand. We may not be adulterers or liars, but any spot upon us separates us from the purity of God. The filth of sin covers us the same way it did David. When we sin we need to be cleansed immediately or our sins will begin to pile up until we are buried in them, as David was. Recognize your sin immediately, be honest about it, repent before God and let Him wash you clean. When you sin you must make a choice. Ask yourself, "Do I take this sin to God and let Him wash me clean, or should I just be quiet and work it out myself?" David made his choice and found the answer the hard way. Let go of your pride and let God wash you, because you can never do it yourself. The alternative only brings pain and suffering.

Accept the Only One Who Can Cleanse You

God made him who had no sin to be sin for us, so that in him we might become the righteousness of God (2 Corinthians 5:21).

Just as the Jewish priests did when they put their sins on a lamb's head and sacrificed it as a sin offering, God put all our sin on Jesus—all the dirt, bacteria, fungi, germs, and evil—and sacrificed Him on the cross. John the Baptist recognized even before Jesus' death that He was the Lamb of God (see John 1:29, 36).

How can we present ourselves before God as pure and innocent? Jesus, the Son of God, took upon Himself, as the Sacrificial Lamb, all our sins and carried them to the cross. When He defeated death by His resurrection, the debt was paid. Death washed Jesus clean of all our sin that He carried. Sin was defeated.

The results of sin's defeat are monumental. We now have a way to have sin washed away from our spirit. This bridges the separation we have from God. It gives us an opportunity to be seen as worthy of eternal life. When we accept that Christ carried our sin to His death, God no longer sees the sin we carry, only the Sacrificial Lamb that took it away. As Paul said, God sees not us in our sinful state but sees us through the righteousness of Christ.

A wise friend described it to me like this. When God judges us after we die, He will look to see if we have any sin on us. Fortunately, Jesus will step in front of us and He will be all that God sees. This is what John was talking about in 1 John 2:1: "I write this to you so that you will not sin. But if anybody does sin, we have one who speaks to the Father in our defense—Jesus Christ, the Righteous One." Imagine! Jesus is our advocate who defends us here on earth before Almighty God, the Judge; He paid the ultimate penalty for all our transgressions with His death; He continues to speak for us in heaven, defending us from the accusations of the Evil One! As the old hymn says,

Hallelujah! What a Savior!
Hallelujah! What a Friend!
Saving, helping, keeping loving,
He is with me to the end.[3]

With all of the world's sin washed from Jesus, our Advocate, God will never see a speck on us. God will have no other option except to judge us as worthy of eternity in His kingdom.

However, there is a catch. This can only happen if we choose to accept this great Gift, accept His sacrifice, and accept His daily guidance. We will then have all sin cleansed from us. There is no shower hard enough, sponge big enough, or cleanser strong enough that we can use to wash and become clean through our own efforts. God needed Jesus to sacrifice Himself and destroy the power of sin. No one of us has the power to do that. God wants to take care of us. His desire is to wash away all harm and evil from our spirit. He wants to close the chasm between us and create intimacy instead.

Throughout the history of mankind God has been trying to save His creation. First it was through the Law; now, since Jesus, it is through grace. Many, through faith in God, have accepted His way to salvation, letting Him wash away that which separates us from a Holy God. The book of Hebrews lists some of those the Old Testament tells about: "All these people [a great cloud of witnesses surrounding us, now in heaven] were still living by faith when they died" (11:13). Many who were alive when Jesus walked the Earth witnessed the sacrifice of Jesus. Many others looked forward to the Messiah's return. In any case, the Bible is full of examples of God cleaning out sin and changing lives. These examples clearly illustrate the effects and consequences of sin. More importantly, they illustrate how a loving God wants to cleanse us and relate to us. But there are right ways and wrong ways for us to seek His cleansing.

Whitewashing the Outside Doesn't Help

Cleanse me with hyssop, and I will be clean; wash me, and I will be whiter than snow (Psalm 51:7).

This psalm also comes from David's encounter with Nathan the prophet. David saw his deep need to be cleansed from his sin and knew God alone could do that. David could wash himself, looking clean to the world around him, but

God would see through to the truth. David knew that he needed to be cleansed at the spiritual level, enduring the process of renewing his heart. He wanted to be whiter than snow and be pure in the sight of God, once again.

Many people know they have done wrong but look for a way to appear clean and fool people. This may be a great temporary fix, but eventually the shine will fade. At some point, the strain of pretending will become too much and nobody will be fooled anymore. Unlike people, God cannot be fooled or manipulated. God knows what lies within our hearts and will not be pleased by our acting. In fact, Jesus was clear about those who pretended to be clean in His day.

The Pharisees were a religious group of Jews whom Jesus rebuked often for trying to fool men. In Matthew 23:27-28 Jesus rebukes them by comparing them to burial tombs that were customarily painted with whitewash to appear clean, despite the death inside. Jesus exposes them as wicked and full of hypocrisy despite their righteous outward appearance. Let us not be seen the same in God's eyes.

Stop pretending you are okay, trying to appear clean to others. Merely washing the outside to cover the dirt inside you is fruitless. In the end, you will only be holding yourself back by wasting all your energy on an act. After all, you cannot fool yourself. The real pain caused by the sin in your heart will eventually wear down and ultimately destroy your spirit. If you want to truly know peace and live free from guilt, you must allow God to wash you. Only that deep spiritual washing can bring you to purity. David knew it and wanted his psalm to help everybody else know it.

The phrase, "Cleanse me with hyssop," is taken from a section of Old Testament law dealing with leprosy. Leprosy is a rare skin disease today, but prevalent in those days. Basically, the skin of a leper decays over time, even to the point where they lose fingers, toes, and other appendages. The worst part is that it is very contagious. Passed from person to person it can devastate large groups of people.

The law dealt with leprosy in great detail. David used a part of the law that described the process of cleansing a person healed of leprosy. In Hebrew Old Testament custom, after a full examination by a priest, blood would be sprinkled on a leper with a hyssop branch. It was the final declaration that they were no longer contagious and were disease-free enough to rejoin their community.

Looking at it symbolically, leprosy can be seen as a spiritual condition caused by sin. Over time, left untreated and able to spread, the condition will worsen and eventually—moment-by-moment and piece-by-piece—will erode your spirit. It will kill you. It is what holds us back from reaching our full potential to

God's work. The disease takes away our strength and often keeps us going backwards. It is more contagious than leprosy and can affect many. Spiritual death in one can change the attitude and effectiveness of whole groups. I have seen churches and organizations affected dramatically by leprosy. Because one of their leaders infected a whole congregation, the church lacked strength and ability to grow.

It is different than physical leprosy in one respect. It is not visible to others. It lives on the inside, away from human eyes, slowly destroying our spirit. Like those whitewashed tombs, we can appear fine on the outside but be secretly dying inside. This spiritual leprosy can only be seen by God and our self. Because of this fact, there is only one way to get free from it. Let God wash it away from us.

The death of Christ gave us the tools we need to be washed, but they must be used. We need our High Priest, Jesus, to cleanse us with His blood. The effect of allowing God to cleanse our leprosy is a very profound one. As the verse says, we will become "whiter than snow." Snow is possibly the purest form of water. We can be completely purified from our sin and, greatest of all, pure in God's eyes. The key to this purity lies not within our power, but with the power of the God of eternity.

The priest had to be the final judge of a healed leper. God wants to declare us truly clean once and for all. A true healing will mean that the leprosy will not return. It will mean that we are ready to serve with the strength we have regained. So let the High Priest cleanse you by the blood of sacrifice. He will sprinkle you with a hyssop branch. You will be whiter than snow, totally washed, clean, and pure.

Being Washed Is a Daily Activity

Jesus answered, "Unless I wash you, you have no part with me" (John 13:8).

The disciples and Jesus meet for the Passover supper, Jesus' last supper. The disciples are unaware that the next day will be the last for Jesus. Before they share supper, Jesus confuses them by wrapping a towel around His waist and filling a basin with water. The disciples are bewildered as He begins to wash their feet, the humbling, dirty duty of a servant. A servant would be required to wash the dirt from the master's feet after a journey. It was a dirty, unwanted, and thankless task, to say the least.

On the surface, this seems like a lesson of servitude, but I believe it goes far deeper. This lesson is usually misunderstood because our modern minds cannot conceive what life was like two thousand years ago. The people of that time had no shoes, only sandals or bare feet, and travel was done on foot, on dirt paths, so their feet would have been filthy. It was absolutely a must to wash their feet to stay healthy. It would be very different for Jesus, their leader, to wash His followers' feet. So when Jesus comes to wash Peter's feet, Peter wants no part of it. Peter thinks he should be washing the feet of his master. Jesus rebukes Peter saying that he must be washed to be any part of Jesus' ministry. Peter relents, understanding his need, even asking to have his head and hands washed.

The great question, then, is why would Jesus perform this act of a servant? Well, the answer is simple; Jesus *had* to wash their feet. The disciples had to understand what it really meant to be washed clean.

Throughout the Bible, feet are symbolic of the way an individual lived; clean feet were a sign of righteousness. The dirt on feet was symbolic of the sin picked up from the world. Basically, feet are our point of contact with the world. If we live as part of the world, we will be dirty. If we are washed, it is evident that we are with Jesus. Jesus was teaching that He had to wash away the dirt of sin or it would pile up, leading to infection and decay.

We have to find a way to live in this world without being dirtied by the sin that is everywhere we look. The truth is, we cannot avoid sin; only keep it from affecting our hearts. No matter who you are, your sin is making you filthy. The question then comes, "How can that sin be washed from my heart?" Jesus' act of service is our answer.

Before your sin can pile up, allow Christ to wash your heart with the water of the Holy Spirit. This is not a one-time procedure, the disciples had to wash their feet often. No matter how hard you may try to avoid it, sin will happen to you. You have to step up and honestly deal with it, face to face. What sin is piling up and dirtying your heart? You can try with futility to wash yourself, but unless you let Christ do it, you can never have a relationship with Him. In this verse Jesus said, "Unless, I wash you, you can have no part with me." Accept what God is offering you right now and join the work of His kingdom. If you want to be part of what God is doing and will be doing, get washed!

"You Must Be Born Again" Comes First

He saved us, not because of righteous things we had done, but because of his mercy. He saved us through the washing of rebirth and renewal by the Holy Spirit (Titus 3:5).

So how, then, are we saved and able to appear clean before God? It is only by His mercy. He knows all of our deep needs and cleanses away our sin. God washes us with the Holy Spirit, giving us a new standing before Him. It is not enough for God to clean you on the surface. He wants to tear away the sin that clings to your heart in order to regenerate and renew your whole being. It is like our bodies that need to be cleansed daily. Every day dead skin cells pile up and we need to use soap to remove the dead skin and dirt, so that our bodies can regenerate a new layer of skin. God must remove our sin to allow the Holy Spirit to regenerate and renew our spirit. Then we can stand before God. The Spirit is like our spiritual soap. He changes us from dirty, filthy sinners into saints that are able to change the world.

Peter told his readers that if they were to look forward to their home of righteousness they would have to make "every effort to be found spotless, blameless and at peace" with God (2 Peter 3:14). That cannot be done in our own efforts; it must be done through the cleansing power of the Holy Spirit.

You can be totally new; a new creature with new thoughts, attitudes, words, and actions. Sounds like a great opportunity to me.

So, What Is the Process?

I will sprinkle clean water on you, and you will be clean; I will cleanse you from all your impurities and from all your idols (Ezekiel 36:25).

Ezekiel was a prophet whose ministry took place entirely during the exile. God had allowed the Babylonians, led by King Nebuchadnezzar, to capture the Jews and take them back to Babylon. Many would endure imprisonment, slavery, religious persecution, and worst of all, the destruction of Israel. This time of exile and captivity would last seventy difficult years. Ezekiel's ministry started five years after the exile. At that time, he was only thirty years old. God called on him to write this book and prophesy to the nation of Israel. Ezekiel's words were met by desperate ears and this verse speaks to them.

The Bible explains that God had allowed the Jews to be in captivity for seventy years because they had broken their covenant with Him. The Jews had forsaken the Lord and followed idols. Many prophets had been sent to warn Israel but were often ignored or violently stilled. Their sin had become so great that God allowed an attack on them and everything they loved. God wanted to get their attention, hoping that one day they would give Him their trust once again. God wanted them to remember how much He loved them and had done for them. If they did that then God might be willing to covenant with them once again. The point here was not about what happened in the past between God and His people, but how God would renew their future. Ezekiel was explaining exactly what God wanted to do when the Jews finally returned from their long exile in Babylon. God wanted to rebuild the nation not only through reconstructing buildings, but reconstructing their relationship with Him. A new Israel would allow God to start over and the Jews to go back to their first love. God knew that in the past His people were full of sin and disobedience. God also knew how much He loved them and wanted to be with them. His kindness and mercy would renew their standing with Him. God does the same thing for us over and over again. He knows all of our faults but loves us just the same. He is always there to renew our relationship.

God is more than able to step into our lives even when we are filthy with sin and clean us to the heart. Even when we, like the Jews, have broken our relationship with God; when we have trusted in idols like time, money, material things, and desires; when, over time, we have become separated from God; when we have become dirty through contact with a world that has held us captive; even when the relationship God wants with us has been torn down to the last strand; even in those moments when we are lowest, because of God's great grace, mercy, and wisdom, there is a prophet calling out to us. The Holy Spirit is shouting out to us the message of a future of renewal and regeneration given to us by God. The message is loud and clear and full of desperation. We can have all our filth and sin washed away. An old, dirty, rotting past replaced by a new, pure, fresh future.

If you look within and know that your idolatry has led you from where you belong and taken you as a captive slave, separating you from God, please come back. Someone once told me that if you were one hundred steps from God you only needed to take one step back. He would take the remaining ninety-nine steps towards you. Take that simple single step and you will experience something amazing. God will wash you with pure water, forever renewing your future.

If you have wandered away from the cleansing power of the Holy Spirit, return to where you once lived with God; the place He gave to you out of love. If you have never been there and have never had a relationship with God, know that you were intended to live there. The point is not where you have gone or where you started but where you choose to go now. When you return and once again place God first, He will cleanse you.

God's greatest desire is for us to allow Him to cleanse us so we can renew our relationship. It is like a shower that is always on. The opportunity to become clean is always nearby, but as ridiculous as it seems, many forget that it only works if we get in and get wet. Every one of us will become dirty from time to time, but God is always there, waiting for us. He wants us to come and allow Him to pour water down upon us and make us clean. All the sin, idolatry, and disobedience that have dirtied our past will be washed off, fading off into the drain, never to be seen again. We can come out of the experience totally new and once again able to connect with God the way He intended. So go ahead. Get in and get wet.

"Now Is the Time of God's Favor" (2 Corinthians 6:2).

If we confess our sins, He is faithful and just and will forgive us our sins and purify us from all unrighteousness (1 John 1:9).

Paul, in his second letter to the church at Corinth, quotes Isaiah when he said, "in the time of my favor I heard you, and in the day of salvation I helped you." Then he says, "I tell you, now is the time of God's favor, now is the day of salvation" (2 Corinthians 6:2).

The Apostle John, in his first letter, described what God can do for us. Every single person on this earth has sin in their hearts and lives. What separates a child of God from everyone else is how he or she deals with his or her sin. God is calling every one to lay down sin and confess it to Him. God knows the sin that lies within every heart, but cannot help until we choose to give it to Him.

Only when we come to a place where we let go of our sin, does God have the power to completely remove it from our hearts and lives. John promises that God will do that. God cannot go against what He has promised, so the choice is ours to make. If we take up His offer He is allowed to work. Not only can God forgive us for our sin and how it hurts Him, but He can also wash us clean from it. It is one thing to be forgiven, which ends the pain of consequences, but having our guilt washed away erases the pain entirely. Psalm 103:12 describes the complete effect by saying that "He has removed our sins as far away from us as the east is from the west."

Let's look at it from a modern perspective. In our system of laws, forgiving someone who has broken the law cannot remove the crime from his record. A murderer can receive forgiveness from a victim's family, but the consequences of the crime will remain. The sentence given by the judge will not change. Imagine that things were not that way and that through forgiveness, that murderer's crime would have no sentence and even be erased from the record. How much more would forgiveness mean to a truly sorry criminal. The effect might be powerful enough to totally change that person. Believe or not, God really does that for us in the court of eternity. God not only forgives us, but will also take away the sentence of death. Even more, He will forever remove our crime from the record. I don't know, but that might be enough to change someone. It sure changed me.

God will wash away our sin and shame forever, but we must come to Him as we are, still covered with our sin and ask Him to prepare us to stand before His presence. If we do not have the proper pass we cannot appear before an earthly king. Neither can we appear before the Heavenly King without the proper pass—the cleansing "blood of Jesus, his Son," that "purifies us from every sin" (1

John 1:7). We want to appear clean before the King, and may seem that we deserve it. Forget about it! Why not just come as you are to the cleansing power of the Holy Spirit?

You can try to avoid what God wants to do in many ways. You may find forgiveness from another human, but God alone can wash away your sin. Are you willing to carry your shame in defiance to God? I urge you now to confess the sin in your heart and allow God to be faithful. Then He can forgive you and wash it away from your record:

Peter Marshall, the former chaplain of the United States Senate, loved to tell a story called "The Keeper of the Spring." This simple tale beautifully illustrates the importance of constantly maintaining the purity of our hearts.

> An elderly, quiet forest dweller once lived high above an Austrian village along the eastern slope of the Alps. Many years ago, the town council had hired this old gentleman as Keeper of the Spring to maintain the purity of the pools of water in the mountain crevices. The overflow from these pools ran down the mountainside and fed the lovely spring that flowed through the town. With faithful, silent regularity, the Keeper of the Spring patrolled the hills, removed the leaves and branches from the pools, and wiped away the silt that would otherwise choke and contaminate the fresh flow of water.
>
> By and by, the village soon became a popular attraction for vacationers. Graceful swans floated along the crystal-clear spring, the mill wheels of various businesses located near the water turned day and night, farmlands were naturally irrigated, and the view from restaurants sparkled.
>
> Years passed. One evening the town council met for its semi-annual meeting. As the council members reviewed the budget, one man's eye caught the salary paid the obscure Keeper of the Spring. "Who is this old man?" he asked indignantly. "Why do we keep paying him year after year? No one ever sees him. For all we know, this man does us no good. He isn't necessary any longer!" By a unanimous vote, the council dispensed with the old man's services.
>
> For several weeks nothing changed. But by early autumn, the trees began to shed their leaves. Small branches snapped of and fell into the pools, hindering the rushing flow of sparkling water. One afternoon, someone noticed a slight yellowish-brown tint to the spring. A few days later, the water darkened even more. Within a week, a slimy film covered sections of the water along the banks, and a foul odor emanated from the spring. The mill wheels

> moved slowly; some finally ground to a halt. Businesses that were located near the water closed. The swans migrated to fresher waters far away, and tourists no longer visited the town. Eventually, the clammy lobe due to fingers of disease and sickness reached deeply into the village.
>
> The shortsighted town council had enjoyed the beauty of the spring but underestimated the importance of guarding its source. We can make the same mistake in our lives. Like the Keeper of the Spring who maintained the purity of the water, you and I are the Keepers of Our Hearts. We need to consistently evaluate the purity of our hearts in prayer, asking God to reveal the little things that contaminate us. As God reveals our wrong attitudes, longings, and desires, we must remove them from our hearts. [4]

Quickly, the embarrassed council called a special meeting. Realizing their gross error in judgment, they rehired the old keeper of the spring, and within a few weeks, the veritable river of life began to clear up. The wheels started to turn, and new life returned to the hamlet in the Alps.

This story is a very powerful one that I go back to time and time again. It says that no matter how useless you may feel or how little worth other people see in you, we are all important. Even if it is unseen, we play a vital role in God's plan. If we do not play our role then God's system will work badly or not at all. We are not all called to be missionaries or preachers but God will use all of us in one way or another. I remind myself of that when I feel discouraged or worthless. I know that God may want to use me at any time, so I must be prepared and believe that anything can happen, even through me.

Esther was an average Jew under the rule of a Babylonian king who prepared herself and believed that she had a great purpose. The amazing thing was that she became a great queen and used her power to save her people. Her uncle reminded her, "Who knows? Maybe you were made queen for just such a time as this" (Esther 4:14). Within a very short period of time Esther's circumstances changed from seeming hopeless to one of the most important events in the history of the Bible. The bottom line is that no matter how useless we may feel our purpose can become evident in the blink of an eye.

4

Walking

I can't walk, as some of you may have figured out. It isn't much of a Sherlock Holmes mystery. This fact is probably what affects my daily life the most. It means that I need another person to lift me in order to move to or from my chair. Up until age eight, I was able to walk on my own. At that time I began using a three-wheeled scooter to help me go long distances. That scooter aided me for a short time, about a year and a half. Some time during my tenth year, I lost most of my mobility. I became in total need of the scooter to get around any distance and, of course, someone had to pick me up and carry me from place to place—to and from my bed, my toilet, my shower, the car.

I was at the age when independence is extremely important. And mine was being taken away. Other kids were still walking, running, climbing, skating, playing games. I had to be carried everywhere I went! It was the ultimate lack of independence.

Moving on our own is taken for granted and becomes second nature. I was forced out of that way of thinking and humbled by my need for help to move. It was difficult, but I was able to push beyond it, and live my life.

All of this happened very quickly. In only three and a half years I went from a normal, walking, six-year-old to a completely dependent ten-year-old. Yes, I know that I had a disease, but it was hard to get used to so quickly.

Things have not changed in this area of my life. I still need to be carried everywhere. That's the way it is. What has changed, however, is how I view it. I see it as a chance to see things from a different perspective. I will say it again: the one word that describes what it is all about is *humility*!

Humility is a scary idea because it means being honest, and being honest often makes us vulnerable. Vulnerability breaks down pride. Yet, becoming humble clears the way so that we can help ourselves or others. Being carried by others is my ultimate exercise in humility. Humiliation is more than just a risk to me. And

I don't get used to it. It hits me every time someone new helps me. What if I get dropped? Do I look like a wimp? Macho people don't need to be carried!

I have not been dropped yet. And nobody has accused me of being a wimp. I still worry, but I cannot let it overcome me. If I did, I would never allow myself to be moved and would be stuck in this chair all the time. Then I never would gain the blessings that humility brings: relationships with others. I believe that people gain more by helping me than I do from them. If I do not allow someone to help me I rob them of any learning and growth they may receive.

This is how we should live as Christians. We are in need of being carried when times are tough. Those times when we are carried are the times of greatest growth and humility. Being independent teaches us nothing about God, others, or ourselves. The good times are great, but we never learn as much as we do during the bad times. Our pride can only turn into humility when we are vulnerable. If we walk alone when we most certainly cannot, we rob God, others, and ourselves the rewards of humility.

In my mind, being carried has a greater reward for God and others. I say this from true experiences. Someone at a summer camp once told me, "Thank you for letting me help you. I was a little intimidated by you when this week started, but now I realize you are a cool guy. I never would have known that if you hadn't allowed me to help you." That statement is still powerful to me today and it should help you see how humility helps other people. There are times when you need to humble yourself and allow another person to carry you. Yes, it can be scary. You are vulnerable to rejection or being dropped. However, doing those very things will develop much closer relationships.

One of the purposes for the community in a church is to help us grow in humility. One person helps another, knowing that we all need help—right now or will eventually. The power of a church body lies within the relationships developed through humility and vulnerability. Simply going to church on Sunday and shaking a few hands will never develop relationships. Only by allowing others to carry you will you know real strength. It may seem risky, but the reward is far greater.

The rest of this chapter will deal with how God carries us and what His reward is for carrying us when we allow Him to.

I want to share a great example of what I am talking about. This story is well known, but it is worth repeating because it expresses how God works with us.

> One night a man had a dream. He dreamed he was walking along the beach with the Lord. Across the sky flashed scenes from his life. For each scene, he

noticed two sets of footprints in the sand; one belonging to him, and the other to the Lord.

When the last scene of his life flashed before him, he looked back at the footprints in the sand. He noticed that many times along the path of his life there was only one set of footprints. He also noticed that it happened at the very lowest and saddest times in his life. This really bothered him and he questioned the Lord about it. 'Lord, you said that once I decided to follow you, you'd walk with me all the way. But I have noticed that during the most troublesome times in my life, there is only one set of footprints. I don't understand why when I needed you the most you left me. The Lord replied, "My precious, precious child, I love you and I would never leave you. During your times of trial and suffering, when you see only one set of footprints, it was then that I carried you." [5]

Why Do We Need to Humble Ourselves Before God?

Humble yourselves before the Lord, and he will lift you up (James 4:10).

God wants us to be humble, vulnerable, and open with Him. It may be scary to open up and be vulnerable with God for a couple of reasons. What if He requires something of us that we don't want to do? And what will others think if we fail? How humiliating! That is pride! And it is something we have to get over.

If we do not humble ourselves before God He will be unable to get close enough to bless us. That is what this verse means. If we allow ourselves to be open and vulnerable to God despite the risks, He will be able to lift us up and bless us. You must *allow* God to pick you up when you cannot walk; however, He will not do it against your will. If you do not allow it you will be stuck right where you are. And think of the blessings you will miss!

The key to dependent living is seeing your need and then asking for help. I could lie in bed all day long, being stubborn and refusing help, but I would not do anything except stay in bed. Probably, a few people would try to make me get up. I could lie in bed day after day, never participating in the joyous life God has for me, getting up only when the sheets had to be changed. But I choose to humble myself and let others—and God—get the most out of my life that I can give.

The Dead Sea in Israel is a great example of this. Rivers and streams flow south into of the Sea of Galilee, keeping the sea fresh and full of fish. Then they emerge as the Jordan River and continue flowing into the Dead Sea, where the water stops and stagnates. The area around it is very salty, so the sea is full of salt (and this is not the "salt of life" Jesus talks about) and other minerals. The salt keeps away life. Plant life is practically non-existent. It is far better to be like the Sea of Galilee, full of life and hope, than like the Dead Sea, stagnant and rotten so that nothing can grow and develop within us.

Don't become stagnant in life, unable to move past your current state. Let God carry you to the next level. The only way to reach higher is if God brings you there. Pride is what keeps us from reaching to God. It is the complete polar opposite of humility and can have a devastating effect on our lives. We can remain stagnant and secure for a time but soon we begin to rot.

God has called us to be full of life. Jeremiah 17:7-8 says, "Blessed is the man who trusts in the Lord and has made the Lord his hope and confidence. He is like a tree planted along a riverbank, with its roots reaching deep into the water—a tree not bothered by the heat nor worried by long months of drought. Its leaves stay green, and it goes right on producing all its luscious fruit" (TLB). This is the effect of God carrying us. We can be always growing and fruitful when we trust the Lord.

Humble yourself to the Lord, allow Him to pick you up despite the possible humiliation, and He will lift you from where you are stagnating to where you can be full of life, love, and fruit. He can have direct access to your heart so that you can then be blessed and grow in Him. Otherwise, you are eliminating God's ability to help you mature and grow stronger.

A Humble Person Is Ready to Be Led

Lead them like a shepherd and carry them forever in your arms (Psalm 28:9, *TLB*).

This verse speaks very well to the ability of God to carry us past any obstacle that may be in our way. It also shows another aspect of God's character. He is our Shepherd and He will take care of us, because we are part of His own flock.

The job description of a shepherd is very simple: lead the flock to where they can find food and water, keep them from danger, and give them freedom to roam. The lambs need to grow and develop into mature sheep. The Good Shepherd will do whatever it takes to make sure those things are available to every one of His sheep. There are times when the shepherd may be called upon to protect the flock. Other times a shepherd must gently help a weak, powerless sheep to keep going. This is the aspect of a shepherd this verse focuses on.

Every person goes through times when they feel weak and powerless. It is in those times when we need God the most. The Apostle Paul says, in 2 Corinthians 12: 10, "When I am weak, then I am strong." Those moments we feel the weakest are when God will step in and carry us. Weakness is definitely looked down upon in our society today, but in God's eyes, weakness allows Him to do what

He longs to do. When a sheep was too weak to keep going, unable to walk and keep up with the flock, the shepherd would have to carry it. God wants to do the same thing for us.

But, as I have said many times throughout this book, God will not intervene on your behalf unless you ask Him to. God wants you to make every decision. Many people are rendered weak and helpless because of various circumstances and sins, but their pride will not allow them to let God carry them through. If I were to allow my pride to take over, I would never move from my present position. I would simply lie in bed or sit in my chair and nothing would ever change.

How long will you stay stuck in your present position? God is waiting for you to give Him the access He needs to carry you to a new position. He sees your weakness and wants more than anything to carry you and be the one you rely on.

Sometimes We Need to Be Carried

He tends his flock like a shepherd; he gathers the lambs in his arms and carries them close to his heart; he gently leads those that have young" (Isaiah 40:11).

A flock of sheep is made up of lambs that are not mature, adult sheep that only need to be led to green pastures, and those who are self-motivated. Here, again, we see how God shepherds us, no matter where we are in maturity.

The lambs cannot fend for themselves; they are unable to find food on their own and need help. These are the babes in Christ who often need older sheep as well as the Shepherd to mentor and protect them. The brand new ones often need to be carried.

Those sheep who are maturing need only protection, as Paul described them, from "savage wolves" that will not "spare the flock" (Acts 20:29), and food. Once they have adequate food they can pretty well go their way under their own power, but still be ever watchful of the wolves. Finally, there are those to whom God gives responsibility because they can motivate themselves. They have grown past needing to be fed and carried. They only need to be shown how to take care of that which God has given to them and they will do it. This is the picture of the aggressive ram that will attack an enemy that threatens the flock until the shepherd arrives to help.

These three groups are at different levels, but one thing remains the same, they all need a shepherd. God desires each one of us to become mature within the flock. God wants us to get to a place where we do not need a lot of help to follow the shepherd. Being mature in this case does not mean that we become independent from God, but we know how to follow the shepherd. We have learned to recognize our Shepherd's voice and to follow him because He is the Source of our strength.

When we first make a commitment to follow the Good Shepherd, we are not mature enough to truly know how to follow. Our hearts are in the right place, but we are not yet experienced enough to go it alone. Like the lambs in this verse, we may stray into dangerous situations without knowing it, or we may fall down. This does not mean we are going to remain this way, but we need the Shepherd to carry us at various points in our walk. When we allow God to carry us we gain deeper maturity and an understanding of how to follow God. God carries us when He wants to teach us what it truly is to be like Him.

Once we reach a certain point of maturity, God may give us the responsibility to take care of something for Him. God has seen fit to give us a task that will benefit the Kingdom. But here again, we cannot take complete responsibility for this task, for this is the time when we need God the most. The task we have been given can easily become a distraction and lead us away from the Shepherd. We need God even more to lead us and show us the way. God will slowly walk in front, carrying His staff of protection, so that we will not lose track of Him while we are dealing with great responsibilities.

The point is that no matter what level of maturity we reach, we still need God to help us. Maturity is not a reason to move away from God, it is a reason to move closer. We all live within the flock and are led by the same Shepherd.

God Has Promised to Be Faithful in Carrying Us

Listen to me, … I have created you and cared for you since you were born. I will be your God through all your lifetime … I made you and I will care for you. I will carry you along and be your Savior (Isaiah 46:3-4, *TLB*).

This verse is saying something very simple, but the circumstances surrounding it illustrate a deeper message. Throughout most of their Old Testament history, the nation of Israel had rebelled against God by following other gods. God was very patient with the Israelites for many years but eventually gave up trying to fix the broken contract. God would no longer offer His protection. He allowed Israel to be taken captive by an enemy nation, Babylon. This captivity lasted for forty years. It ended when God moved the king of Babylon to let the Israelites go.

Isaiah was a prophet who gave God's message during Israel's long period of captivity. The people were at their very lowest point and desperately in need of God. Israel had lost everything, their wealth, their kingdom, their power, and worst of all, their connection to God. Things were as desperate and desolate as they could be, but God was still there. God promised to carry them through these terrible times. He promised to end their captivity and renew their stature.

Everyone goes through these terrible times, times when it feels as though everything is lost. I have gone through times when it felt as if there was no hope, but I knew that God was still there for me. He wants to pick us up as His children and shelter us from the pain. We all want a daddy to hold us when we fall down, a daddy to wipe away the tears when we cry. Come to Him when your need is great and He will be that daddy. Let Him carry you through those bad times. Let Him carry you through the worst times of hopelessness and despair. No situation is so great that He cannot carry you through it.

Sometimes, as it was with Israel, the days of captivity are brought on by sin. Israel made a choice to forsake God and break their contract with Him by following other gods. Our sins may not be as drastic, but they probably helped lead us into our current desolate circumstances. This is a great example of the consequences of living in independence. Our sin tells God that we don't need Him or want Him. Eventually, God will step back and leave us free to live as we want to. This may seem good for a time, but without God's protection we will be open to attack by our enemies, the raging wolves. Satan, the world, and even our own desires can take us captive. God is like a shelter in the wilderness. If we stay within Him we will be safe from the elements. If not, the cold, the rain, and the wind will get to us. Which choice is the wisest decision?

If you have been enduring the pain of being taken captive by an enemy there is an escape. The solution to this problem is simple; turn your independence into dependence. God ended the Israelites' captivity in Babylon only when they had shown that they were once again dependent upon Him. You cannot escape captivity or change the circumstances around you without being reconnected to God. It is only when you let God carry you that you will gain your freedom. To shift from captivity to freedom you must shift from independence to dependence.

Keeping that in mind will not eliminate the bad times, but it will help to shorten them and give you peace in the midst of the pain. Jesus told a story about a person who built a house on solid rock. When a storm came and tried to bring destruction onto that house, it stood firm and strong. On the flipside, another person built a house on sand. When that same storm came and tried to bring destruction onto that house, it fell with a mighty crash. Jesus was saying that God would give you what it takes to make it through. Hold tight to God and let Him hold tight to you and you will survive.

We Need One More Virtue

Humble yourselves, therefore, under God's mighty hand, that he may lift you up in due time (1 Peter 5:6).

We still need one more action to assure our walk with God is strong. This verse is sort of a bottom line for this chapter. God is teaching us how to have a real relationship with Him. This is what I have been talking about this entire chapter. Humility is the most important aspect of our life as a Christian. It is the realization that we are incapable of doing anything without the aid of God. We can have faith that when we rely upon Him in humility His strength will lift us up and make us stronger. We know that God's hands are mightier than we can even fathom. Giving up and relying on God's strength makes us more powerful than we could possibly imagine.

Right now you may be thinking that this is a really good deal. Humbling yourself in order to gain God's strength may even sound easy. However, there is a bit of a catch to this. Humility must be practiced daily, because it goes against the way we are wired. Pride is an enemy that always wants to rob us of the strength available in God's mighty hand. Pride will say that we do not need God's strength; that we have enough strength within to do what we need to.

Beyond understanding that humility is difficult, there is another catch within this verse. The catch is the last part of that says, "in due time." Patience is a requirement beyond humility. I have often missed this step myself. The power that God grants us through humility is not an instant power-up. God alone knows the right times when we need this power and strength. In our society, we want things now; it's called instant gratification. But God sets His watch and lives by His time. We have to give God complete control to get His strength.

God wants us humble so that when the time comes to utilize His strength, we will give all the glory and honor to Him. Pride will instantly destroy all that God has done through us. This is why patience is so important. Being patient is our way of telling God that everything we do is because of Him. God wants us to mix the formula of humility and patience just right so that He can work through us. Once again, not only must we realize our need for humility, we must cultivate it, proving to God that we truly need and want His help.

5

Breathing

This disease has also diminished the ability to breathe on my own. First I had to utilize a machine called a BiPap to breathe effectively enough to sleep through the night. I now use a ventilator to help my lungs inhale to full capacity. I am very thankful for the equipment that has been provided to me, but to be honest, it was very hard to accept that I needed these things.

From about the age of fifteen I knew the time would come for me to rely on these machines. I put this very real future in the back of my mind in an attempt to avoid it. I did everything I could to not think about it until a series of events in 1998 forced me to face it.

In December of 1997, my family and I went on vacation to Disney World. During the trip, I noticed my appetite decreasing dramatically; I wasn't eating as I usually did. During the flight home I became very sick to my stomach and had to use an airsickness bag, if you know what I mean. These two events, combined together, started me thinking that something bad was happening.

Soon after arriving home, I became more and more ill. I was barely able to eat anything and got very little sleep. I would toss and turn all night, sometimes needing to turn about thirty times. All of these things caused my family and me to feel as if we were at the end of our rope. We visited our doctor who dealt with Muscular Dystrophy at Children's Hospital in Seattle. He was less than helpful. The extent of his evaluation was to look at my tongue and skin. He sent me home that day with a tube down my nose into my stomach to give me nutrition. We were kind of shocked that he simply brushed off what was happening.

A few days later it was apparent that I was not improving. I then visited my family doctor who could not believe the state I was in. I had lost thirty pounds, now weighing about sixty-seven pounds. Right then he called a doctor at a higher level of responsibility at Children's Hospital and explained what had happened. Dr. Kraft told us to come to the hospital and check in that day.

Upon my arrival the doctor once again had a feeding tube inserted to my stomach to stop any more weight loss. That night my doctor also set up a sleep study to find out why I could not sleep. Blood work showed that I had severe problems caused by dehydration. The study and blood work revealed some startling news. My weight loss and lack of sleep was due to my lungs being able to fill only 25 percent of their capacity. Suddenly all the thoughts that I had been pushing away became a reality. In order to compensate for this lack of oxygen I needed a new breathing machine, the BiPap. This machine blew air into my lungs every time I inhaled, aiding me to reach full capacity and breathe effectively all night.

After being informed about how bad my situation was, the first doctor visited me in the hospital. He apologized, but the damage had already been done. I no longer worked with him after that because I felt he did not care enough. The whole experience taught me to trust my body more because people make mistakes. Doctors may have more education, but they are still human.

The painful reality that I could no longer breathe on my own was easily outweighed by the great results I was getting. In about two months I was sleeping well and gained back the thirty pounds I had lost. Once again, however, I had been forced to let go of another ability, another piece of my independence.

About three years later, in 2000, I was dealt another blow. In September, I came down with a really bad cold. I believed I would get over it just as I had other sicknesses in the past. By the beginning of October, I was still dealing with that cold. One afternoon while I was using a machine to help me cough, some of the junk got stuck in my throat, cutting down my breathing. The ambulance was called and once more we went to the hospital. On the way I lost consciousness. When I came back around I was aware that I would need more help breathing if I were to avoid getting sick again.

Previously that year my lung doctor told me I would soon need help to breathe during the day as well as at night. I did not like what I heard. However, soon after that ordeal that sent me to the hospital I realized that I would have to deal with this new loss of control. Soon I was set up with a ventilator, a system that pushes air into my lungs when I need it. It basically allows me to inhale fully. At that point I pretty much had full reliance on machinery to help me breathe.

Once again, learning to rely on breathing equipment to live a quality life taught me more about relying on God. God helps each person to breathe spiritually, giving them life both literally and figuratively.

God's Breath Brought Life to Adam

The breath of the Almighty gives me life (Job 33:4).

This statement in Job is very powerful. God has to give us the air and breath we need every day to be healthy; we cannot do it alone. God's breath sustains us and gives us all we need to live. Without air in our lungs and the ability to breathe it in and out, there is no life for us. But that is not all the air we need. This is also very true in our spiritual life. Something must help us each day if our spiritual life stays healthy.

Through His Holy Spirit God gives us the spiritual air that we need to live. The Spirit is God's power to us here on Earth. In John's Gospel Jesus called Him "the Counselor," or in the *King James Version*, "the Comforter." I can tell you that having help to breathe physically was a great comfort to me. Being able to utilize the Holy Spirit to breathe spiritually is both a comfort and good counsel. We need this power to live the life God has given to us.

We can no more live physically without oxygen in the air we breathe than we can live spiritually without the counsel of the Holy Spirit. The Greek word for Spirit is *pneuma*, very close to the Greek word for "breathe," *pneō* (a word we borrow in the English word "pneumatic," something that moves by air pressure). Yet, how many of us believe we can live a healthy spiritual life without the Breath of God, or try to determine the direction of our lives without this Counselor? We cannot choose to live without oxygen and we surely cannot choose to live without the life-giving Breath of God. Let us not fight this need but instead embrace it as the key to our lives.

Too many brothers and sisters in Christ are spiritually dead because they fight their need for this spiritual "oxygen." An effective spiritual life does not come from following a set of rules or performing certain actions. That kind of life only comes from God's breath giving us the oxygen we need to survive.

God's Breath Will Still Give Us Life

He himself give life and breath to everything, and he satisfies every need there is (Acts 17:25, *TLB*).

God is the ultimate source of both physical and spiritual life. The physical life we live is important, but our spiritual life is of eternal importance. Knowing how important the spiritual life is we must understand where its power lies.

Every facet of our spiritual life has been empowered through God. Every spiritual and physical action we perform, every need we have relies solely on the breath of God. Do you ever wonder why you don't seem to have the same spiritual high other believers have? Do you still have needs that are not satisfied? Maybe it's because you have not allowed God to give life to what you do. When we accept this "breath of God," the guidance of the Holy Spirit, all our needs are taken care of.

When we attempt to breathe life into our spirit by works or by our own strength, we find that it has no power. No amount of reading the Word, or doing good works, or going to church will strengthen your spiritual life or satisfy your need without the intervention of the Holy Spirit of God. True satisfaction and power come only from the Lord. Trying to do it by yourself will reward you with small, temporary, satisfaction and power, but complete satisfaction and power are found only in the breath of God.

God's Breath Can Restore Life in Us

This is what the Sovereign LORD says to these bones: I will make breath enter into you, and you will come to life. I will attach tendons to you and make flesh come upon you and cover you with skin; I will put breath in you, and you will come to life. Then you will know that I am the LORD (Ezekiel 37:5-6).

This verse is a great illustration of what God is capable of doing. If we ever reach a point in life where we feel spiritually dead God can breathe life into us once again.

Every one of us has made mistakes here and there that have hurt us spiritually. We may have even neglected our spiritual life for a time. Mistakes and neglect can damage or starve our spirit even to the point of death. Even those who have the very closest relationships with God can feel dead. Thankfully, God has the power to revive our spirit and set us once again onto the course to life. We can make hundreds of mistakes, and neglect our spiritual life for hundreds of days, but God can erase all of that with one breath.

God is so full of life His every breath gives life to the entire universe. His breath was the power behind the resurrection of Jesus. That same breath is the power we need to resurrect a dead and powerless spiritual life. Why would God do this for us after we neglect His great power? Because He wants us to know that He is Lord, the true source of life. When we experience the life-giving power of His breath for ourselves there will be no denying it. God is what we need now and all we will need forever. He alone is the giver of both spiritual and physical life. He wants you to know this to enable you with the power to live the life He wants you to and with the tools you need to do whatever task is before you.

6

Surgery

I have gone through several major surgeries to help improve the quality of my life. This is one of the more intense aspects of living with Muscular Dystrophy. While the surgeries have surely been needed they came with a great deal of anxiety and apprehension—they endangered my life. The nature of these procedures combined with my fragile health made the stakes considerably higher.

There are risks involved with any surgery, but in my case, the risks are multiplied. People die on the table in surgery. Yet, despite the uncertainty, avoiding surgeries is often not an alternative. Avoidance would be profoundly worse.

Without the surgeries the quality of my life would now be miserable and the length of my life drastically decreased. In the end, the surgeries have had great rewards because they make my life today much better.

Now I would love to tell you that the surgeries I had were easy and came with little discomfort; that would be the farthest thing from the truth. Despite the ultimate, final rewards, recovery was often very miserable. The many bumps in the road led to times of depression. Each experience was, at the same time, life changing but very difficult.

In 1988, my brother Jason and I visited the Muscular Dystrophy clinic in Boise, Idaho. A doctor informed us that I would soon need major surgery to correct a problem with my legs. Lack of muscle use creates what are called "contractures." These contractures cause an imbalance between muscles on opposite sides of a leg, foot, arm, or hand. The stronger muscles, usually the inner ones, begin to take control. In my case the inner muscles of my feet forced my feet into a pigeon-toed position. Surgery, which required cutting into the Achilles tendon, would release the pull of the stronger foot muscles, allowing my feet and legs to straighten again.

Despite knowing that the surgery was very necessary, I felt a lot of apprehension and anxiety. I really wanted to avoid it. So that is pretty much what I did for the next few years. During that time we moved from Idaho to Washington State, which allowed me to keep surgery on the back burner.

In early 1990, surgery was no longer avoidable; my need for it became terribly apparent. Since surgery was scheduled for November it would have a major impact on my family and school. As the date approached, I felt more and more anxious about the process. The surgery itself was not going to be a big problem; the recovery was. It would be long and hard.

When I came out of surgery I discovered a full cast on both legs reaching all the way to my hips. A stick between my knees connected the two casts. I had not expected that, and it ended up giving not only me but all around me quite a bit of misery.

The casts were uncomfortable and made it very hard to sleep; I had trouble staying in any position for long periods of time. The experience was horrible for my family and me. I wish I could offer some sage advice and encouragement to any of you who might be facing this ordeal. The truth is that it became a daily battle just to stay sane. One day at a time became more than just a cliché. It was real rough but the rewards did outweigh the costs. The surgery saved me a lot of pain down the road. I have seen the results of those who avoided this leg surgery. Their feet and legs are turned at gruesome angles, causing a lot of pain. I know that they would have chosen differently had they known the later effects.

One year later, I was visiting a clinic at Children's Hospital in Seattle and we were informed of my need for another important surgery. This surgery would be quite dangerous and recovery as tedious as before. Sitting in the same position in my wheelchair for years had caused scoliosis. Scoliosis causes the spine to curve laterally at varying degrees. My case was urgent and I needed correction very soon.

The surgery would be very invasive. Two stainless steel rods would be inserted on either side of my spine and would be attached by a wire woven between each vertebra. The process of tightening the wire would straighten out the scoliosis. It would be a very dangerous six-hour procedure. We were told that death was a very real possibility and had happened before.

To say the least, this news was an eye-opener for all of my family. While we knew I needed the surgery, the thought of going through another major recovery was hard to take. However, avoiding the surgery was not an option. Without it, the scoliosis would worsen and put me in a near ninety-degree lean. Positively, it would add at least ten to fifteen years onto my life. So without much debate we scheduled the surgery for September of 1991. The thought of this surgery brought the same kind of apprehension as the others had, but the fear was increased. I knew that it would be much more difficult and dangerous.

After surgery, I remained in the hospital for about a week just getting past the pain and becoming strong enough to start recovery at home. I experienced a lot of soreness as my body got used to having so much metal inside. It took about three months to get back to some state of normalcy, but my body reacted well to the surgery and the scoliosis was completely corrected. It was a very hard three months but, looking back, I advise anyone in my situation to go through it. Lengthening life by up to fifteen years is worth all the pain and discomfort

When I was first diagnosed with Muscular Dystrophy at the age of six, I was only expected to live to be eighteen. The greatest aspect of enduring these difficult surgeries and recoveries was the reward of a nearly unlimited life; that is the point of any surgery. Despite the pain and arduous recovery, a better quality of life can be expected for those who endure them.

Unfortunately, fear keeps many from the great rewards that lie ahead. Fear tells us to keep everything in our lives the same, take no risks because of what might happen. However, those same risks often have great rewards lurking behind them. I know people who have let fear tell them to avoid these surgeries until they are absolutely necessary. By avoiding an inevitable procedure, surgery and recovery become more difficult. I have learned that if something painful results in the reward of a better life not to hesitate to take on the possible risks. Face them head on!

Spiritual surgery brings the same apprehension and fear as physical surgery. Such surgeries are sometimes painful, the recovery time very difficult. But the rewards are worth every bit of it. These surgeries also involve risks and unknowns. God desires to change our lives for the better, but not without risk. We need to be vulnerable, allowing God to bring us through the painful process of spiritual change, and then gain the eternal rewards He has presented.

Many say they know God but never allow for change. Yet we all have some spiritual problems that can be corrected only through invasive surgery. Fear has kept many a person from facing that truth. The longer a person waits to face the difficult process of change, the harder the process will be, and the farther away they will be from reward.

Throughout the Bible God tells us of our need for change. As the surgeon, God can do surgery on our unhealthy spirit and bring in that change, even if it means the incising of the offending part of your life that is contrary to God's leading. However difficult this change may be, with many risks along the way, the reward is always worth it. This change allows us to become closer to the image that God wants us to present. That is what is happening to me.

"Let the Weak Say I Am Strong" (Joel 3:4)

He will take these weak mortal bodies of ours and change them into glorious bodies like his own (Philippians 3:21, *TLB*).

This verse, written by the apostle Paul, was directed to members of a Greek church in a town called Philippi. Apparently they needed a bit of encouragement and clarification. Every one of us has a shared weakness that is unshakable; we are human beings. We are held firmly within the grasp of a curse that leaves us imperfect and leads us along a path towards death, even from the moment we are born. We are mortal and unable to change ourselves. Unfortunately, because of our human weakness, change is exactly what we need.

Paul makes it clear that we are weak and powerless from the very beginning. Our ultimate weakness is being incapable of doing anything good. Each of us, left to our own devices, will willingly choose to go our own way, away from God. God Himself is completely aware of this and longs desperately to change us into what He wants us to be. If we are willing to allow God to give us life-changing surgery, He has all the ability in the universe to do it. As Paul puts it, God will change our "weak, mortal bodies" into glorious heavenly ones.

Our need to be changed may be a hard fact to swallow. Yet there is no getting away from it. The good news is that, like the surgeries that were available to lengthen my life, the Great Physician is available to fix our weakness. He has a surgical procedure that will change us completely and give us a better life, one He intended for us all along. He wants to mold us into something that looks like Him.

To be totally fair and honest, this surgery also has some bad news; it will be difficult and full of pain. It hurts to give up most of what you have and much of who you are. God cuts out everything in His way, those parts of you that are not responding to His idea of perfection. Some of those parts have grown roots; they cannot be removed without causing damage.

Like any other surgery, there is risk. You must become vulnerable, trusting the Surgeon with your life. But remember this: there is no reward without risk. The reward is a life transformed, filled with quality, strength, and power.

Being transformed into glory means that you experience a tremendous amount of change. Change is always difficult but spiritual success depends on it. It is unfortunate that the knowledge and fear of pain and difficulty is too much for many to bear. It keeps them from going through with the surgery. It is a large price to sacrifice everything, but those who recognize how desperate their need is gladly lay their life into the Surgeon's hands.

Paul is trying to say that whatever the cost, the reward is worth it. We will be weak and mortal no longer. We will be glorious and strong; able to move closer to what God wants us to be. Without the surgery of transformation we will stay the same; incapable of doing good. We will remain evil and selfish, trying to go our own direction. That sounds pretty bleak to me.

Unlike the questions and fears I first encountered upon hearing the diagnoses concerning my physical surgeries, in my mind there is no questioning my need for change in my spiritual life. All of us, absolutely, without a shadow of a doubt, need God to transform us. God challenges us to become as great as we can be and, in the process, become as glorious as God intended us to be.

"What Counts Is a New Creation" (Galatians 6:15)

And no one pours new wine into old wineskins. If he does, the wine will burst the skins, and both the wine and the wineskins will be ruined. No, he pours new wine into new wineskins (Mark 2:22).

The power in these words of Jesus lies within their symbolic nature; they show our need for complete change. The new power God has given us requires something new to contain it. The old container simply does not have enough space or strength to handle it. Making a mistake by putting God's great power into a weak and unchanged heart will only create a spill, leaving that heart empty and torn. God must dwell in a place strong enough to accommodate Him.

Mark, in this verse from his Gospel, paints an interesting picture, both literally and figuratively. In the time of Christ, drinking water was a rather risky proposition. Because wine goes through a process of fermentation it is purified. It was much safer to drink than most water. Because wine had so much value to so many people wineskins were very important. A wineskin is a bag made of animal skin meant to, of course, store wine. Over time, wineskins expanded because of the weight and fermentation process of the wine. This expanding made an old wineskin unfit to contain new wine. If poured into an old, stretched out wineskin the pressure would build as the wine fermented and that, combined with the weight, would make the bag burst.

I have a friend who told about a church her husband started in a tent in Phoenix. They used to store the leftover bottle of communion grape juice behind the piano until the next month's communion service. One Sunday morning, after a particularly hot spell, they went into church and discovered the very strong smell of wine. The grape juice had begun to ferment and expand, and soon burst the capped bottle containing it. It was several days before the tent was wine-free again.

The wineskins represent our hearts. Our hearts are no different; they are spiritual wineskins. Over time they become stretched out and hardened through the sin and pain of this world. A heart in that condition cannot contain God's power. We must get a new heart. This transplant is not an easy process and requires major surgery. God must reach down deep into our souls, tearing out the things we have grown accustomed to being attached. This process is very painful because it requires us to let go of all that we have become. Our new heart must be directed toward God. It may seem like the most terrible process, but in the end we will have the strength and ability to be what God wants us to be.

Many people choose not to cut off those attachments of their hearts. As a result, the offending parts maim, cripple, and expand like tumors threatening their lives, leaving them in desperate need of an emergency heart transplant. This is much more painful because God has to perform emergency surgery. Things must be fixed very quickly.

Do not avoid what you desperately need to be: a container that holds what God wants to give you. As James says, "Come near to God and he will come near to you. Wash your hands, you sinners, and purify your hearts, you double-minded.… Humble yourself before the Lord, and he will lift you up" (4:8, 10). Let your heart be replaced with something much stronger, giving you the capability to follow God.

"Power Through His Spirit in Your Inner Being" (Ephesians 3:16)

Though outwardly we are wasting away, yet inwardly we are being renewed day by day (2 Corinthians 4:16).

This verse is a great summary of what it means to follow God. It also gives us insight into how exactly we are able to follow Him. As humans we are made up of two basic parts or sides; an outer, mortal, imperfect part that fails us constantly and an inner, eternal part that strives and longs to be at peace with God.

Our outer part is dying, and has been since birth. This outer part wants nothing to do with God. It is sinful, lustful, and cares only for gratifying its wicked human needs. God cannot bear to see our awful outer part. God cannot change that part of our human nature. He is more interested in that part of us that needs Him.

Our inner part is, by nature, not much better than the outer, but it can be changed. When our outer part—our hands, feet, and eyes, as Jesus said—leads us to sin, the inner part feels the effects. The emotional pain and emptiness of sin is a product of our inner part, our heart, knowing it is distant from God. Our inner part wants and needs God to intervene, creating change.

God will do that if we allow Him to surgically repair our inner being. This surgery cleans up all the damage done by the outer being and renews our inner part. There is no hope for the bodies we all possess; only the heart and soul can be repaired and renewed. Our bodies constantly cause damage to our hearts. This damage is done every single day. God must renew our inner being day by day. He must perform surgery daily, and it is vital because the inner being will decay and die without renewal. When the inner being dies it kills our connection with God. God wants to remain connected to us. We all must choose daily to allow this surgery so that we can remain with God.

Will we do whatever it takes to follow God or will we let our connection with Him die?

7

Living

What is it like to live with a disability? What can you expect to happen? How can success be found where it doesn't seem possible? These are some of the questions people ask about life, whether they are disabled or not. I will try to answer some of them from my point of vies.

It was 1984. I was a six year old visiting a medical specialist in Denver, Colorado. The doctors ran a few tests and even performed a muscle biopsy on my thigh, cutting out a piece of muscle to test. The results of these various tests revealed something quite startling and unexpected. The words that poured forth were as powerful as a warning about the fury and destruction of an oncoming hurricane.

"I have some really unfortunate news." My family and I were informed that I had a form of a genetic muscle disorder called Duchenne Muscular Dystrophy, named for its discoverer Guillaume Duchenne. We also learned at that time that my younger brother was also afflicted with it. And like hearing that hurricane warning, it was met with disbelief because there was no evidence of its devastation. We had no idea what the true effects would be on my and my brother's lives. The hurricane was coming, like it or not, and it was going to do damage.

Muscular Dystrophy is a genetic disorder that affects a muscle's ability to regenerate and become stronger. Within every muscle cell there is a protein called "dystrophin." This protein keeps a muscle cell together, giving our muscles the ability to increase in size and strength. In simple terms, it is the glue that puts muscle cells back together after they have been stretched and torn through exercise. My muscle cells are unable to utilize dystrophin, causing them to lose strength and eventually be destroyed. At the time of my diagnosis the disease had a terribly daunting outlook. We knew all of my muscles would be affected and that the disease would eventually take my life.

At the time, it was impossible for me to grasp fully with my naïve childish understanding, but the news must have been devastating for my family, my mom especially. Every parent dreads the knowledge that their child's life will be anything less than they envisioned. How do you accept that your child will know suffering more than other children do? It was very difficult to swallow.

Muscular Dystrophy would cost much of my brother's life and mine, changing it for sure; the prognosis was brutal. We were told not to expect living past our teen years. Being that I had the mind of a six year old, I had no concept of what was going on. I did know that there was something wrong with me.

Quite a few incidents had led us to believe that there was a problem. About a year previous to my diagnosis, the daycare I attended had a banquet for parents. I felt so proud that my mom was there and I wanted to make her happy. I wanted to go and get food for her by myself. I remember loading her plate, knowing that I would impress her. As I was carrying the plate to her, I tripped. The problem was that nothing caused me to trip. I tripped because my muscles could not hold me up. All the food I was carrying went everywhere and I was totally humiliated.

This isolated incident would not have much meaning if it were not for the fact that I was tripping on a nearly constant basis. I distinctively remember a time when I was not able to play at the same level as the other kids. I would get very frustrated because I could not go at their pace and would always fall down. It soon became obvious that I needed medical attention. Our doctor observed that I did have some sort of issue and sent us to a clinic. The doctors at this clinic were the ones who performed my biopsy and ultimately diagnosed me with Muscular Dystrophy.

The worst part about Muscular Dystrophy is that no cure currently exists. Since the age of eight, I have been completely confined to a wheelchair, unable to walk. Over the length of my life I have lost nearly all ability to help myself. I have the same function as a quadriplegic. This condition has nearly destroyed my will to live several times. I know that this disease's sinister, murderous, rampage ends with death.

I am not being overdramatic, that is the truth. It is a horrible disease with a terrible amount of power over my body. But its power ends there! It cannot touch my mind, soul, or spirit and that is who I truly am! My identity is about much more than having a disease. Truth be told. this disease has been a gift. It has made me sit down, slow down enough to see things others don't. I have insight and vision into the deep important things of this world. I am forced to live life with a raw, intense, honest view of the world and those who live in it. I am forced to constantly examine all of my life and myself, the good, the bad, and everything in between. I am keenly aware of my limitations. But this knowledge frees me to put all of myself into what I can do.

Despite its best efforts, I have refused to let this disease take complete control of my life. It has destroyed much of my physical abilities, but the often difficult and painful road I have traveled has taught me lessons others will never learn. Spiritually and emotionally, I believe I am stronger than those who possess all their physical abilities.

Unfortunately, learning these lessons has come at a great cost. I've missed out on many experiences others realize. My school years were very difficult on me. As I grew up I was constantly reminded of being different: living in a wheelchair; facing children and adults who did not treat me well or truly understand my life; depending on other people for every basic need; facing the prospect of death at an early age. Although I was not expected to live past the age of eighteen I am now twenty-seven (at the writing of this book).

Almighty God, advances in the medical field, improved medical equipment, and surgeries have added many years to my life and given me a nearly unlimited future. Remembering the good and the frightening events in my life are the foundation on which this book is written. To see where I'm coming from I must bring you through the most important ones. You, the reader, must relive my experiences to truly understand what I am saying.

My childhood memories, as early as daycare, were the beginning of my understanding that I was different. Despite that understanding, growing up in an apartment in Colorado Springs, Colorado, I had the same childhood experiences as anybody else. I was a snot-nosed, troublemaking brat who harassed his brother. I lived a pretty normal life until I was in the second grade, unable to walk anymore. I needed a wheelchair to get around.

My first wheelchair, as I have said, was a three-wheeled scooter called a Pony; it seemed more like riding an untamed mustang. Before I learned to handle it I would take a corner with too much speed, and the rodeo was on. I battled head-to-asphalt on a playground and lost. The scooter fell over on its side and nearly dumped me out. When I finally became used to running the scooter it was an important aid in my daily life. I no longer struggled with basic mobility issues; I could go where I wanted and do what I wanted much more easily. It was great, but I now had to deal with some other issues. I was completely different from all the kids around me. I experienced a few tough moments with a few bad kids, but lucky for me, most kids dealt with me very well.

From 1987 to 1989 we lived in the ski resort town of Sun Valley, Idaho. It was a great place to live in the summer, but winter was hard, especially on a wheelchair. Throughout the winter, the snow easily piled six feet high, not exactly wheelchair accessible. My brother and I really had no way to get around at all. I had to accept once again that my disease would keep me from doing many of the things others could enjoy. The older other kids and I grew, the farther apart we became. As we grew out of childhood activities I stayed home more as they went out more.

In the summer of 1989, my family made a major move to Olympia, Washington. This change introduced me to one of my favorite teachers. He was my fifth grade teacher, Mr. Hughes, and he was also disabled. He helped me forge the attitude I have towards my disability. Mr. Hughes was an amputee without his right arm. Seeing how another person dealt with their disability on a daily basis helped me see that I was capable of doing many things despite my limitations.

Because of the experience he had with his own disability, Mr. Hughes never made things easier for me. He treated me just as he treated everybody else. This was a great help to my relationships with other students. Now nobody treated me as if I were different. I am very blessed to have had such positive experiences in school. I know many other disabled people who had a much more difficult school experience.

Until high school everything went relatively smoothly. With the exception of a few bad experiences, I had no problems with students, but now I faced a few barriers from administration. When I started high school as a freshman, their solution to handicap access was to create a cutback between two different sidewalks. So naturally, on my very first day of high school I turned onto the cutback and fell into some bark mulch. To my great embarrassment, the students who helped me up were all seniors. My cover was blown. Instead of being anonymous I became a sympathy case.

One major problem was getting from the classrooms to the gymnasium. The classrooms were on an upper level with a ramp that I could roll up on. Going down was a real rush. There were stairs inside the building for the students to get to the gym. But I had to go outside the building to get there. Olympia, Washington, is not like Phoenix. We often have cold and rainy weather. My health is very fragile in the winter and being outside was the worst risk I could take.

My parents went to the school board meeting trying to get a better solution to our problem, an elevator. The board refused to listen; their new solution was to make another sidewalk skirting the outside of the building with rails that made it safer. The solution was great, except that I still had to go outside to get from one building to another, with no cover. So we hired a lawyer and forced a meeting with some of the administration. We told them of our real need for an inside elevator. We told them forcefully that I could get very sick. Apparently, putting legal pressure on them was exactly what we needed to do. Almost immediately they made plans to install an elevator.

The fight we had was startling because we had never faced such opposition. The administration was against us nearly from the very beginning. The whole experience taught us to fight for what we needed no matter what barriers we faced. I believe that experience taught me a lot about facing opposition. No one will keep me from achieving my goals!

Each experience—bad or good—that I faced during my school years taught me lessons. I learned that being different was not such a bad thing. I learned that many different people would come across my path giving me mostly good experiences, but sometimes bad ones. Life is all about facing different situations; and how you handle it, what you learn from it, is all that matters. Most of my life has been filled with various hardships, forcing me to think about important things that most never ponder.

Depending on other people has made me think about what humility is all about. It is not difficult for me to be vulnerable because I have been vulnerable all of my life. People can live their whole lives and never truly be humble or vulnerable.

I am very aware of my needs and capabilities and have learned exactly what I can and cannot do. Our politically correct world keeps many people from analyzing their weaknesses. As a result, they never fully understand how to utilize their strengths. True success and satisfaction comes only from being weak, humble, and vulnerable. In order to be aware of our strengths our weaknesses must be laid bare. Honesty is the key. The prospect of death has made me understand and live out a productive life. You must take advantage of every opportunity, no matter what it is or how many you encounter. What you do is way more important than what you have.

There are many spiritual and emotional lessons every human should learn but many feel no need to. Those people generally never think about what they have learned until they are dying, then it is too late. Their lives have been empty and fruitless. Successful people are those who think about the truly important parts of life; my disability has given me an opportunity to do that. My desire is to help others think about what is truly important and figure out how they can have this kind of success.

These lessons I have learned through my physical difficulties have a more eternal, spiritual meaning. I am writing to you to show how these physical lessons I have learned can be translated into spiritual lessons, spiritual lessons that can have great implications upon anyone's life, whether or not you are disabled.

My ultimate goal is to teach you how to find true success and satisfaction in life. Those wonderful things can only be attained through a relationship with One who is greater than we are. As I am physically dependent on others, we must all be spiritually and emotionally dependent upon God Almighty. Only He can give us all we need to succeed. The Bible is very clear about out dependence upon God to give us life.

Stay Connected to the Vine

I am the vine, you are the branches; if a man remains in me and I in him, he will bear much fruit, apart from me you can do nothing (John 15:5).

This illustration Jesus gave His disciples has more power and depth than meets the eye. It is enough to build an entire life upon. This is exactly what God wants in any relationship with Him, one that is far closer and more intimate than the deepest relationships we have ever experienced. Marriage is the most intimate relationship we know, but it is only a foggy view of real intimacy, leaving room for selfish independence. A relationship with God is so much more fulfilling. Let's analyze this verse and help you grasp its power.

Jesus was probably thinking about a grape vine. The vine and its branches are different from each other but bonded together deeply at their core. Branches are totally dependent on the vine to live; apart from it they will die. Branches can do only what the vine directs them to do, spreading out in the way that is best for the vine. At the same time, a vine can live without certain branches; it simply grows new ones. However, without branches, the vine is limited. It can climb upward but cannot reach outward in all directions. Branches need to be connected to a vine to live and a vine needs its branches in order to reach out. God looks at us as branches that are attached to Him, the Vine.

We need God an awful lot more than He needs us. If we are to live we must be attached to Him. Once a connection has been made, whether through a natural outgrowth or through being grafted in, we become capable of bearing the fruit for which we were created. Being bonded to God allows Him to direct where we go and what we do. God has total control, He can do with us whatever He knows is best for His kingdom and for us. This idea makes many people uncomfortable, but I know that God can organize a life better than a thousand of us combined can do.

If we become detached we will die, so we must work diligently to stay connected and alive, receiving nourishment from the Vine. Like any good vinedresser knows, branches must be cut back occasionally to stimulate maximum growth. This is called pruning, an essential activity that cultivates the relationship's potential. We can do self-pruning by cutting out all that keeps us from being close to God and receiving the nourishment we need to grow strong, nourishment such as a consistent prayer life, directly communicating everything we think, feel, do, need, want, or desire to God. We get this nourishment from the Vine when we read, learn about, and understand everything God has spoken to us in His Word, the Bible, and by showing and giving God affection with worship, declaring His greatness out loud.

Being a branch is a big responsibility. Maintenance is difficult and never, ever completed. You never hear anyone give a branch credit for a bountiful harvest of grapes. Giving a steady effort with very little recognition, appreciation, or reward takes perseverance and humility. Despite that, nothing you can comprehend or imagine is better than an intimate relationship with God. Working for God, the Vine, gives our every action eternal significance, not only for ourselves but for others as well. Only God can reach out and fill the void inside us with satisfaction and fulfillment. It almost seems unfair to receive these things from God with such an eternally small cost and sacrifice.

Why would such a great and powerful God do such great things for weak and powerless people? God will do whatever it takes to get close to His most prized creation, His sons and daughters. He wants the connection to be strong enough that He can be part of everything we do. He wants to be within every breath, touch, taste, smell, sight, and sound we experience. A strong vine produces strong branches that, in turn, give back to the vine nutrients and oxygen. The branch lives only to help the vine. You can experience the fullest life imaginable if you are willing to give up your life for the growth of God's kingdom. We all long for a relationship so full of love that we would give up our lives. No relationship is stronger or deeper than that. God is waiting for you to take hold of His hand and walk with Him for eternity.

The following Scripture, from *The Message,* is longer than I have quoted thus far. But it is sort of a "globe" that helps us see the entire "world" rather than one "country" at a time. This powerful event in the life of the Apostle Paul is a great example of the entire process it takes to transform a spirit.

> *All this time Saul was breathing down the necks of the Master's disciples, out for the kill. He went to the Chief Priest and got arrest warrants to take to the meeting places in Damascus so that if he found anyone there belonging to the Way, whether men or women, he could arrest them and bring them to Jerusalem.*

He set off. When he got to the outskirts of Damascus he was suddenly dazed by a blinding flash of light. As he fell to the ground, he heard a voice: "Saul, Saul, why are you out to get me?"

He said, "Who are you, Master?"

"I am Jesus, the One you're hunting down. I want you to get up and enter the city. In the city you'll be told what to do next."

His companions stood there dumbstruck—they could hear the sound, but couldn't see anyone—while Saul, picking himself up off the ground, found himself stone blind. They had to take him by the hand and lead him into Damascus. He continued blind for three days. He ate nothing, drank nothing.

There was a disciple in Damascus by the name of Ananias. The Master spoke to him in a vision: "Ananias."

"Yes, Master?" he answered.

"Get up and go over to Straight Avenue. Ask at the house of Judas for a man from Tarsus. His name is Saul. He's there praying. He has just had a dream in which he saw a man named Ananias enter the house and lay hands on him so he could see again."

Ananias protested, "Master, you can't be serious. Everybody's talking about this man and the terrible things he's been doing, his reign of terror against your people in Jerusalem! And now he's shown up here with papers from the Chief Priest that give him license to do the same to us."

But the Master said, "Don't argue. Go! I have picked him as my personal representative to Gentiles and kings and Jews. And now I'm about to show him what he's in for—the hard suffering that goes with this job."

So Ananias went and found the house, placed his hands on blind Saul, and said, "Brother Saul, the Master sent me, the same Jesus you saw on your way here. He sent me so you could see again and be filled with the Holy Spirit." No sooner were the words out of his mouth than something like scales fell from Saul's eyes—he could see again! He got to his feet, was baptized, and sat down with them to a hearty meal.

Saul spent a few days getting acquainted with the Damascus disciples, but then went right to work, wasting no time, preaching in the meeting places that this Jesus was the Son of God. They were caught off guard by this and, not at all sure they could trust him. They kept saying, "Isn't this the man who wreaked havoc in

Jerusalem among the believers? And didn't he come here to do the same thing—arrest us and drag us off to jail in Jerusalem for sentencing by the high priests?"

*But their suspicions didn't slow Saul down for even a minute. His momentum was up now and he plowed straight into the opposition, disarming the Damascus Jews and trying to show them that this Jesus was the Messiah (*Acts 9:1-22*).*

Paul's story illustrates how drastic the change must be in order to transition from false independence to total dependence. It shows that the perceived independent, strong, selfish person is indeed weak and powerless and in desperate need of support. It indicates how if we utilize that support we will find true satisfaction and success.

No matter the person, that transition is always shocking and difficult. Paul's experience was spectacular; I guess God had a hard time getting his attention. Whatever the method, the results were amazing; a murderer became the most prolific writer in the New Testament. It is a great encouragement to know that if God can turn around such an evil spirit, dealing with us is a piece of cake.

It is ironic that Paul became physically blind because of his spiritual blindness. He lived his life blind to the true nature of his spirit, blind to his need for God's help. Everything was about Paul. His heritage, training, knowledge, lifestyle, and beliefs made him selfish, arrogant, and ultimately, misled. He described his position in Philippians 3:5-6, "Circumcised on the eighth day, of the people of Israel, of the tribe of Benjamin, a Hebrew of Hebrews; in regard to the law, a Pharisee; as for zeal, persecuting the church; as for legalistic righteousness, faultless."

None of these things impressed God in the least. After all, He is the Almighty Creator of the universe. Paul had come to a point where he believed that he could do everything by himself. He knew God was there, but had no need for His help. Paul was unable to see that the truth was so very far away. God chose to take Paul's sight away to show him the truth. Paul had grown accustomed to relying on himself and his reputation, but being blinded forced him to become dependent on others. A flash of light suddenly changed his perspective; making him aware that all he possessed could easily be taken away. He had to be led around, obviously humiliating to a very proud man; this was God's intention. He wanted Paul to see that his qualifications were unable to help him and that nothing was truly reliable or eternal, it could all be gone in an instant. God wanted Paul to understand that he could depend only on God. The method was drastic and maybe even harsh, but that tremendous event forged Paul's spirit into a weapon more powerful than hell had ever known.

After this experience, Scripture indicates that Saul was no longer Saul but was called Paul, giving him a new identity. Our names are how we identify ourselves, part of the foundation to who we are. To protect witnesses, the legal system often changes identities and names are the basis of that. Our names make us unique and display our connection to family. The Jewish name "Saul," which embodied all that he previously had been and done, was changed to "Paul" to signify his new and unique connection with the Gentiles to whom he was sent.

This is the first time in the New Testament that God chose to become directly involved with the salvation process; He wanted sinners to come by their own free will. But because God needed this man Saul, He had to break into his life and smash down the wall that had been built. The violence of the encounter created a division, totally separating the old and the new. Saul, the independent, prideful murderer on one side, and Paul, the totally dependent, humble Apostle to Gentiles and writer of two-thirds of the New Testament, on the other.

The moment we transition to dependency a change also occurs in us. For most, the transition to dependence is never so drastic; we can choose to change in our own time. Still, it is a very hard thing to face and experience. Seeing disability revealed is a sudden, startling, and even shocking event. We are opened up and laid bare, desperate and vulnerable. To say the least, the first moment I understood what Muscular Dystrophy meant, it was hard to swallow. Immediately, I had a choice to make. Face it and move forward, or give up. Whether or not I was aware of it, I chose the former.

That moment on Damascus Road, Paul had the same choice to make. Get up and move forward in the direction God was pointing him or give up and stay there. In the end, the choice was quite easy; his healing was waiting for him in town. Similarly, I too found a healing on the road I chose to go down. It wasn't a physical healing, but it was what my spirit desperately needed.

Once your eyes are opened and you can see, the sight before you may be shocking. You may see that you are far more disabled and in a far more desperate situation than you thought. Do not fear; remember that in God's eyes, disability is good. It draws us closer to Him, strengthening the relationship we are developing. It is only when we see our disability and rely on God to help us that He can use us. Once Paul realized he was disabled he relied totally on God throughout the rest of his life. He became our most dynamic example of how to walk the walk.

If you see your disability and ask God to help you, think of what you can accomplish. It is a hard thing to endure, but if you head into the direction God is pointing, you will find the reward of a truly successful life.

Let God Mold You into His Image

And yet, Lord, you are our Father. We are the clay, you are the potter; we are all the work of your hand (Isaiah 64:8-9).

God is our Creator and He completely formed who and what we are. Everyone starts out as a lump of clay, as Isaiah pointed out in the verse above. But what we will be is determined by how much we allow God to mold us. God knows exactly how He wants to form someone, but the actions, thoughts, words, and deeds of that person limit what God can create. We must be aware that by living according to God's ways we can be made to look more like what He wants us to look like. Anyone who does not acknowledge this will never be what God intended us to be. We are made to be a container that God will fill with the Holy Spirit so that we in turn can pour out what God has given to us onto others.

But, to be used in God's way we must be filled first. What a wonderful reward! The gifts of God are amazing! They give us power, love, satisfaction, and success not available anywhere else. God must be within us before we have anything to pour out! Once again, seeing our disability and needs actually reveal more strength. The key to the strength of God is weakness. It may not be visible at this time, but I can tell you it's there. God can take useless, formless, disregarded clay and create beautifully formed, useful vessels that pour out God's glory.

I have tried throughout this book to show your deep need for dependence by revealing your disability. We all have a disability; we cannot do anything truly successful or effective on our own. True success and effectiveness are about far more than the shallow view our prosperous society expects. True success is about living above the pain and suffering, being strong when you seem weak and inferior. It is opposite to the modern way of life and thinking.

The television program *American Idol* is a great example of revealing truth to people who are blind to it. It may seem odd and even a little crazy, but I often cheer for Simon. He is brutally honest about talent and may be the first person that actually tells the truth to someone. Too many people come on the show thinking they have a gift when in fact they do not. Viewers often laugh at these people because they look so pathetic. It seems very harsh, but these people need to hear that they need to choose another path or ambition. They have been wasting too much of their life chasing after something unrealistic. They have no talent for singing.

It is difficult to watch someone spend their lives going in a wrong direction. Here is my sage advice in a nutshell: *Find* what you cannot do, then *do* what you can do as well as you can. Forget the politically correct thinking that ignores weakness and embraces effort. Effort is great, but it must be built on truth. *American Idol* paints a very good picture of society as a whole where people believe that their lives are successful, that they are good at something when they really aren't. They just look pathetic and misdirected. They must have their eyes opened to their weakness so they can stop wasting their time.

As long as a person goes around every day without seeing the truth he or she will never see a need for help. Unless you feel a need for God, you will not want Him. Once your disability is revealed, the desperate need for help will become apparent and you will ask for that help and find success you have never known before. God knows your real strengths and how to use them the way they were intended. I like to put it this way: you need to give up so that you can get up.

When you feel you have fallen one time too many you will start to ask why. The answer is simple: you need help! Accept the truth for what it is; don't deny it. Start over, give up doing it on your own and let God rebuild you His way. It may seem odd to get back on the potter's wheel, but you must be remolded. Once you undergo the process of firing you can be filled with purpose, direction, and joy of fulfillment. Despite what other people may think, allow God to help you be what you were intended. Dig deeply into the Vine and receive His strength and direction.

8

Weapons for the Fight

Okay, so now we have looked at the major areas where a spiritual life needs help from God if it is to succeed. By now you should recognize and understand the disabled state you are in and you need to depend upon God in order to live the most satisfying and effective life imaginable.

Finally, I want to take a timeout here to give some much-needed practical advice for those who face Muscular Dystrophy or other physical disability, or, for that matter, any hardship, challenge, or fight you might face.

These ideas come in a few plain statements, but do not be deceived; they are much harder to act upon than they are to talk about. Take a brief look at them here and I will describe them in more detail.

- You and everyone close to you must be completely honest about everything.
- Get to a point of comfort and peace with how you perceive yourself.
- Use creativity and imagination to find solutions to problems.
- Use your strengths to their fullest potential and fight with determination to use them despite opposition.
- Finally, use humor to keep things together and bearable.

If you do these things with passion and tenacity you will be the complete and successful person you were meant to be. Now to show what these suggestions are all about and how you can apply them. Well, I am happy to lead you through them; I believe they will be a great help.

You and Everyone Close to You Must Be Completely Honest About Everything

Many people believe they do this, but most never get all the way to total honesty. Many of us only like the truth that feels good to us. If it hurts we want to minimize the damage. That isn't outright lying but it's no good to anybody. Complete and total honesty includes the truth that hurts and is painful to deal with. It is not pretty or made to look nice; it is exactly the way it is. In my case, that meant being honest about what Muscular Dystrophy was all about. It would take away any sense of the "normal" life I wanted to have. It meant that every part of my life would be dependent on someone or something else. I would live with wheelchairs, surgeries, and have no true independence in the years as a teenager yearning for it. No cars, girlfriends, athletics, or popularity. Difficulty, hardship, and suffering would be around every corner. Ultimately, it meant that death was closer to me than anyone else I knew.

These things were terrible to learn at a young age and were horrible for those who had to tell me about them. As hard and painful as those things were to deal with and to try to find a place of understanding and acceptance with, honesty allowed me to do both. Being honest about what was ahead of me placed a finish line on the course. I had a place toward which I could realistically point all of my effort instead of trying to blindly find my way. The clouds created by dishonesty toward our abilities distort our vision and keep us from getting where we want to go physically and where we must go spiritually.

Why are so many people unable to ever truly find peace and acceptance with what causes them pain and suffering? I believe it is because they either never admit to themselves or are not told by others the complete truth about what they will face. If people do not do this from the beginning, their ability to live with their problems is hindered greatly. Let me give you an example.

If you planned to climb Mount Everest you would be a fool not to look ahead at all the challenges to accomplish such a feat. If you know what to expect you can be prepared. If you do not prepare for everything, you most likely will never be seen again, lost forever in the grasp of the consequences of bad management. Honesty reveals the preparations necessary to climb the mountain—whether it is a natural one or a spiritual one.

I have seen how the lack of total honesty affects people's lives. It creates denial, insecurity, fear, bitterness, anger, and more pain than the original problem was capable of inflicting. Not being honest about the situation will slow the process of finding peace and push others away from helping. Not being honest about a situation makes us appear fake and phony. Most people see through it and, while they may tolerate it in someone who is disabled, they will not sympathize with it. They would rather you were genuine, one who reveals who you really are even if it makes you look bad.

I know a person who exhibits this lack of honesty. I will call him by "Steve." Steve has a disability similar to mine that affects his brain's communication with his nerves, giving him limited body control. Steve makes little or no effort to be honest about it and severely dislikes receiving help to do most things. As a result, he often hurts himself and damages many of his possessions. His lack of honesty affects his ability to get things done well or at all. He pushes away many of his caregivers because when they try to help him do tasks he cannot do himself it reminds him of his needs, inability, and dependency.

Steve has a terrible time understanding that people perceive him differently because of his appearance. While it is not fair that people judge on appearance, that is the way it is in society. When people see him involuntarily jerking about, drooling, and rolling around in his wheelchair they make certain judgments. They doubt his intelligence and stare because he is "strange" and "different." They are wrong, which is sad.

Steve would be a lot better off if he expected this kind of judgment and learned to counter it, to find ways to put people at ease or shake them up a bit. Even though Steve may be angry because this attitude on the part of "normal" people is wrong, he cannot allow that misperception to grab hold of him and perpetuate. Those who judge or stare only feel superior for the moment; then they will walk away and forget it. If Steve were to limit their judgments by being truly honest, he would become even stronger. If he continues to reject his condition it will destroy him.

I have often watched Steve become dangerously angry when others misperceive him, causing great problems in his life, even suicide attempts. When he is unable to get his own way about something he wants to do, rather that just roll with the punches he gets extremely angry. If Steve was honest about his disability he would be much more understanding and might even be able to handle things better.

Steve's lack of honesty goes deeper still. Despite his disability, Steve is very, very knowledgeable in many technical areas. Computers, stereos, televisions, cars, and anything that has power cords, he knows well. This is great except that he often uses this knowledge to cover his insecurity about his disability. When people are awed by his knowledge, his ego bloats and tries to cover his weakness.

I have also known Steve to use many different means to distract himself from the truth. For example, he obtained a great deal of money in a medical malpractice settlement. He spends it on his "stuff," whether for a computer, stereo equipment, televisions, or tech gadgets, then brags about having them. He also uses people's sympathies (especially those of girls), friendly bribes, or his vast material possessions to get others to like him.

I often hurt for Steve because his distorted view of himself leaves him feeling empty and lonely, without peace and acceptance. These feelings are products of his attempts to cover his insecurity. Steve needs the confidence to let others see him in truth and reality.

In order to move on and rise above our problems we must live in absolute reality. No one really wants to live in insecurity and emptiness. But the choice comes down to me. It is up to no one else. I must choose honesty and allow myself to find a point of acceptance and eventual peace. I must know everything I will encounter on the way up the mountain so that I can be fully prepared for the climb ahead. The journey will be painful, dangerous, and terrifying, but the fulfillment of reaching the summit is worth it all.

In 1975, after becoming the first woman to summit Mount Everest, Junko Tabei said, "Technique and ability alone do not get you to the top; it is the willpower that is the most important. This willpower you cannot buy with money or be given by others; it rises from your heart."

Get to a Point of Comfort and Peace with How You Perceive Yourself

Take a moment right now to honestly think about how you see yourself. What comes to mind first? Is it something physical? Maybe a special talent? Did you swell with pride over a great IQ? Or feel embarrassed because you are dyslexic or have some other learning problem? It doesn't matter.

I believe the most important thing here is whether you see yourself negatively or positively. People initially focus either on their flaws or their assets. If you see your flaws first you have already set your sights on failure. Nowhere is this truer than in the world of sports. If a team, or individual, thinks that their opponent is superior to them they will have a very hard time finding victory.

Life is very much the same, but the stakes are much higher. Your path in life is far more important than any game. I want nothing more than for every reader of this book to live victoriously. Your perception dramatically influences the odds for or against you doing that. How you see yourself is entirely under your control and has the most influence on your success or failure. There are countless examples of how a person's image of themselves affects the rest of their life.

My life is no exception. I decided early on that this disability would never define me. I would not allow it to take away any more than it was capable of. I would not grant any extra power to it, would not allow it control over all of my life. This attitude has empowered me and strengthened me every day. Despite its best attempts, I will not let MD win this race; it will never beat me!

MD is always with me, I don't ignore that fact, but it is only one part of me! I know that there is so much more to me than the disability I have—I don't claim it as "my disability." It is not "mine." It has attacked me but it is not me! I am a unique child of God with the power, gifts, and ability to do certain things in an amazing way.

My perception of myself is formed from the knowledge that God does not judge me by the same standards people do. People judge one another on how they look, how smart they are, how much they are worth, what they accomplish in the world, or, conversely, how much damage they do in the world. By most of these standards I will fail others' perception. But if I judge myself by these standards I will feel devastated, humiliated, depressed, and worthless. Other people's perceptions of me are based on things that are temporary and fading. The great news is that God judges me by eternal standards. He sees past what humans see, judging my heart and soul.

Here is a great picture for you. Imagine a scale; hanging from one side is Earth, on the other side is Heaven. The Earth side holds the things people find important—like physical assets and material possessions. The Heaven side contains God's perception of your heart and soul. Which side is heavier? Which side carries more weight? If you answered God's side, come on down and play *The Price Is Right*!!!

Whenever I look at myself I try to see what God sees. Whatever people think pales in comparison to God's view of me. My view, in addition to God's view, gives me the opportunity to find peace and a powerful strength, and enables me to live in victory despite my weakness. The Apostle Paul dealt daily with his weaknesses and wrote this in 2 Corinthians 12:10: "That is why, for Christ's sake, I delight in weaknesses, in insults, in hardships, in persecutions, in difficulties. For when I am weak, then I am strong."

So now what can you do with this? Start looking deeply at how you perceive yourself and rein in the extra power or control that you have given to your weakness. Ask God to show you what He thinks of you. Find a deeper notion of how much power and control you have and shift the odds of victory to your favor. I guarantee that if you combine these ideas you will win the war for the rest of your life. You will never escape your weaknesses, but you can live victoriously in spite of them.

Use Creativity and Imagination to Find Solutions to Problems

Dealing with any weakness on an extended or permanent basis is a very difficult endeavor to undertake every day. I have talked about how to find acceptance with the truth of any weakness you or I might face, but this process is spiritual and rather abstract; it is not tangible. Living daily with a disability or hardship requires some practical ideas and solutions. It also requires us to work with determination to create solutions utilizing our imagination. If we are ever forced into a position where we must do something that we doubt we can do, we must find a solution; I believe that there is always a solution.

I am always put into situations that I doubt I can overcome. If I am in pain, I am determined to find some solution. If I cannot do a physical task, I will try to create an aid of some kind. I go down every avenue available to find a solution. For instance, I have a lot of difficulty driving my chair with cold hands. I could just stay away from the cold and limit my life. Instead, I choose to find a way to keep my hands warm in the cold. My current solution is a sock I have cut to maintain flexibility and a hand warmer packet. This has not helped as much I hoped, so now I am creating a plexiglass cube that will attach to my chair providing a stable, warm environment for my hand.

I could give you hundreds of examples of ideas I have created to overcome obstacles. The point is that I am bound and determined to go to the end of my abilities, not to be limited. This attitude has always inspired me to press on as hard as possible and not quit. I refuse to let my weakness limit me any more than it already does.

Some of you readers may be perplexed by this way of thinking; it may seem contrary to this book's emphasis in some ways. While it is true that we must see our need for dependence and live that way, our limitations and level of dependence are difficult to measure because they are not constants. It is impossible for anyone to clearly know his or her exact limitations; it is not absolute or black and white. What I am talking about is pushing your limits; stretching them to the brink. Because of this gray area you can't sit back, you have to *discover* your extremes. So, give it all you have, body, mind, heart, and soul; don't stop until you have done so. Even if you fail you will live a life full of hope.

The process of creatively using all of your imagination to overcome obstacles is more valuable than the result. In my life, this belief has produced a great sense of hope. I know that I have, at any given moment, the ability to extend my boundaries. Basically, I have the hope and undying belief that anything, *anything* is possible, especially with God as a teammate. This thought can transform your life and your confidence, allowing you to do great things.

Use Your Strengths to Their Fullest Potential and Fight with Determination to Use Them in Spite of Opposition

After understanding and accepting your weaknesses and testing your limits, how do you go to the next level? This part is the most fun and uplifting, where your confidence can be built up the most. At this point you need to discover your strengths, abilities, gifts, and attributes and use them to their fullest potential. Discovering and utilizing your strengths is like bodybuilding, building up your muscles to massive proportions and displaying them by flexing. You can have tangible and measurable results; it doesn't get any more practical. Don't get me wrong though, the process is no piece of cake, requiring quite a bit of work. Becoming Mr. Universe takes a tremendous amount of work and sacrifice day after day after day. Many people don't find success because they don't know their strengths or how to find them. You discover your strengths by looking deep into your heart and listening to many people.

The best way to start is to think about what you enjoy doing the most. More often than not, strengths are tied to what we enjoy doing. Basically, we are wired to do certain things, so if you don't enjoy what you are doing, you are doing the wrong thing and you will never do those things well. If you love talking and dealing with people, you probably have communication skills, confidence, and boldness. If you like being a musician or artist you most likely possess creativity, great intelligence, and vulnerability. The list could go on and on.

A practical way to discover strengths is by taking tests. You can find them on the Internet, in books, employment services, and many other places. These tests I am talking about analyze your personality, aptitude or the skills you possess, job skills, and potential for working at certain jobs. Unfortunately, if taken into consideration individually, these tests have flaws. If you take several, however, a pattern will emerge that you can see. This may sound like a simple idea, but these tests remain an untapped resource that has been neglected far too long.

One of the easiest ways to discover strengths is to utilize insight from friends and family; I don't mean crazy Uncle Joe, senile Great Grandma Gladys, or JoJo and T-Dog. Seriously, they need to be trustworthy, honest, and supportive. Ask your parents, brothers, sisters, close friends, and mature role models, anyone you know who will be dead straightforward honest with you. They know you best and should have a different, outside, objective view of your strengths *and* weaknesses. You might hear something you had never thought of before.

Finally, many of your stronger areas may be hidden and not previously apparent to you. Some say, "I can't do that, I do not have the ability." These same people might later admit, "If I hadn't tried to do that, I would never have discovered this strength." Often, strengths are found under the rocks that have never been turned over; remember the saying, "Let no stone be left unturned?" That is the true definition of persistence and determination. Even if you haven't found your strengths after looking in a million places, continue looking because they might be found in the very next place you look.

Once you have a firm idea of the strengths you possess, you need to utilize them, not lazily, but with full force and determination. Find an arena where you can practice and sharpen your strengths; take control of who you are and what you can do. You now have the ability to push the odds of future success into your favor, becoming the betting favorite. Go out and do whatever great things you were meant to do, influence people, and do the job better than anyone else!

Whoa, hold on a second!!! Don't dive out of the plane with no idea where you are going to land. Knowing your strengths and using them is a great thing, but know that others might not like it and may try to stop you. People may criticize strengths and squelch hopes and dreams. That is the reason you need a powerful understanding and confident grip on the strengths you possess. If you correctly follow the process I have described, you will have an unwavering knowledge of, and confidence in, what you can do. No person should be allowed to shake you up, tear you down, or spin you around. The terrible fact is that some will do whatever they can to discourage you.

Let me give you a personal example of what may lie just ahead. While it is true that I cannot do many physical tasks, I still have much mental strength. I can communicate, lead, write, and work well. While I was helping out my youth group as a volunteer I went to a certain leader and told him that I had been here awhile and I wanted to utilize more of my strengths to help out. I wanted to help lead people and support him the best I could. Immediately, I was told that leaders often do not lead with a position or title; they work in the background.

I thought this was strange because I had observed that the youth had shown difficulty accepting leadership from someone at their same level. I did not want a title, just a position that the youth would accept, respect, and follow; my strength as a leader was obviously in question. My every project to help the group "in the backgrounds" was unsupported; there was apathy over the end result; all my requests for items I needed to complete projects were either filled at a snail's pace or not filled at all. My strengths of creativity, intelligence, knowledge, and organization were severely doubted.

After a year of apathy, questions, and doubts, I moved on. I knew that this person never believed in what I believed I could have accomplished. I know what I can do and I will not allow someone to belittle that. Ultimately, they lost out on what could have been accomplished and I learned not to stay around people who do not believe in and support me.

With this in mind, no one reading this should be unprepared; they should not allow other people's doubts to hurt them. Despite the attempts of the wolves among us to discourage and destroy, continue to propel yourself forward harder and faster.

Use Humor to Keep Things Together and More Bearable

I have been through so very many experiences and challenges, yet one thing has been constant, kept my family on an even keel, and helped life to be bearable. Humor has allowed us to keep everything in perspective and helped us stay level, never getting too high or too low. Humor, to an outside observer, can seem useless and without purpose but to someone who lives with difficulty, the complete opposite is true.

I believe that without humor in my life things would be far too serious for me to handle. I need to find humor to let me see the light at the end of any situation. It may seem strange to some, but if I can't laugh at myself, I can't live with myself. Most people who live well despite a disability or hardship laugh and laugh often.

Hardships can be so deadly serious; we desperately need humor to give light to the dark spots in the picture. Humor is not a form of denial, nor can it be used to avoid reality. It must be used to cope. Humor is a way to put color in a black and white situation. If we live in black and white we will not see all the beauty around us. Black and white makes everything look the same. This attitude piles one brick of discouragement on top of another until the wall looks too high to climb. Humor makes every situation unique. Humor drops each brick of discouragement behind as we go forward, creating a trail that shows where we have come from.

Black and white photos can be great and very powerful, but color brings out the atmosphere, feeling, emotion, and life. Explosions in black and white movies just aren't as exciting. Bright colors make us react with emotion and passion; humor has many of the same effects. When life pushes you to the edge and you feel like you are about to fall, joke about it. When life gets dark, humor can bring light. It may seem strange but laughing at yourself and the situation you are in can be healing. Little else can do more to bring us through pain.

Laughter, as a product of humor, has a profound effect on health in many areas. One of my favorite websites, Howstuffworks.com gives a list of these effects.

- Laughter reduces levels of certain stress hormones.

- When we're laughing, natural killer cells that destroy tumors and viruses increase.

- Blood pressure is lowered and there is an increase in vascular blood flow, and oxygenation of the blood.

- People often store negative emotions, such as anger, sadness and fear, rather than expressing them. Laughter provides a way for these emotions to be harmlessly released.

- Laughter is cathartic, allowing an increase in the ability to cope. [6]

Humor is simple and helpful, but also a skill that can be developed. Skillful humor is knowing how to use it appropriately at the right time and place. It is a skill, in my case, to avoid becoming overly sarcastic. Being sensitive is all you really need.

One of the best examples I have of humor in my life was during maybe the most stressful time I can remember. Earlier, I talked about the leg surgery I had. As I said, we had been surprised about the extent of the surgery. This time was very difficult for my family and me because I was constantly uncomfortable and my sleep was severely limited. Well, during the pain of my cast removal the technician overheard us discussing this lack of sleep. He simply and jokingly said, "Yeah I know, we are *all* tired." It doesn't sound like much, but in the context of the comment we laughed so hard and long that it really took away the stress. For around three months, we continued to use the joke to make us laugh and it really worked. It was a way to put the situation into a form we could handle. We could tuck away a problem for a moment and see the life all around us. Amazingly, as I remember it I am still laughing about it now.

Use humor as often as possible. Take advantage of it as a tool and allow it to be a door to the great healthy effects of laughter. Take the serious, dark, and depressing photo of your life and pour color all over it.

9

Become an Eagle

My youth pastor once told us about the molting process of a certain kind of eagle. Apparently, at middle age, an eagle will fly high, looking for a hole in a cliff. Once it finds the right place it will begin a strange process. First it plucks out every one of its feathers, leaving it bare, defenseless, and unable to fly. But it doesn't stop there. It bangs, scratches, and rubs its beak on the rock until it breaks off. At this point the eagle is a disabled, empty shell of its former glory. After a time of rest, that eagle will regain all of its beak and feather. It will then have more strength.

The purpose of this book has been to take you through the painful process of realizing that you are disabled so that you can be remade into someone stronger. Someone who, with God's help, can face anything and be strong enough to reach the difficult place where true success can be found.

We have exhausted all five of these important processes and ideas. They are much of the foundation upon which my life is built. I have learned these things by going through the fire; they are not objective, outside observations by someone alien to the situation. Ironically, they are just as dependent upon each other as I am on others. Each is separate, but each loses its meaning without the other. These five ideas are essential to moving forward, building blocks that make you capable of reaching the deepest, highest, and most powerful levels you can imagine. One person I know who has taken on and embodied these ideas, using them to propel himself to greatness, who is recognized by everyone with a single, simple, yellow bracelet is Lance Armstrong.

Lance Armstrong has become one of my greatest inspirations; he lives out everything I have written about. By dealing with cancer honestly, he was able to accept it and, going far beyond my suggestions or expectations for any reader of this book, later found a surprising appreciation for it. Lance maintains that battling cancer has made him the spectacular athlete and even more spectacular person he is today. He has found comfort and peace with himself, creating great confidence in who he is and what he can do.

Finding creative and imaginative solutions has become part of his trademark, doing all he can to overcome great challenges and reach victory, not just in cycling. Lance discovered, and continues to discover, the extent of his strengths and often presses them to their extreme limits. He is loaded with an indescribable passion, determination, and perseverance that enable him to reach for and grasp greatness. Humor, of course is an essential element of his life.

On top of all this, or perhaps because of it, his greatness as a seven-time consecutive Tour de France champion is undeniable. He truly has a successful, empowering, influential, and inspiring life. For most, living like this seems miraculous and unattainable but I would bet big money that Lance Armstrong would tell anyone that he is not a superhero, that if they just follow his example anyone is as capable of living with success as he is. Lance has ridden ahead showing us all how to ride well through a life full of steep hills.

Follow the route I have mapped out. It will be difficult, exhausting, painful, and seem out of reach, but the end is worth it. Using the Tour de France as an example, every rider wants to win but is thrilled just to finish the race. They have fought what most deem to be an "impossible" fight against an opponent that is "impossible" to beat and found personal victory. Use this formula and go do the same. With an honest view of your strengths and weaknesses, and the help of God, go out and fight the "impossible" fight against your "unbeatable" opponent.

Some of you may wonder why you need to let God do things for you. Simply put, you, as we all are, are a sinner. We have all broken at least one, and many have broken nearly all ten of the Commandments. Whether just one or all ten makes no difference. According to God's standards we all fall under the title of "sinner." We deserve death. Romans 6:23 says, "The wages of sin are death." But it does not have to be you who dies for your sin. Jesus paid these wages. Without Christ's death on the cross we would be judged under the law.

According to our American legal system, if we break the law we face punishment. Imagine that, before you are to face your punishment, a complete stranger walks in and convinces the judge to allow him to take on the punishment in your place. This is what Christ did for each of us and as the second part of Romans 6:23 says, "But the gift of God is eternal life in Christ." The point is that while we are spiritually disabled and meant for death, God offers us a second chance and eternal life, if we ask for His help. This does not mean He will take away your disability, but He helps you to live despite that disability. God will not take away the same bumps and bruises that everyone else faces, He will help you to deal with them.

My message can be broken down into two simple parts. First, look at yourself and see where you have broken God's law, making you a criminal deserving of death, unable to help yourself. Second, come to God, truly ask Him to help you avoid the death you deserve, and help you to live a full life despite the harshness of this world.

This book is written to five different categories of people:

First, you who have never lived a life of total dependence on God. You have either never known God and have been blind to your need of help from Him, or you know God but never have seen your need for His help.

Second, you who have not utilized God's Bread and Water of Life on a daily basis. You who need to be fed and filled with living water again. You need God to help you eat and drink, to become your provider.

Third, you who need to become humble and vulnerable to God. You have become stagnant and need God to carry you on up ahead and help you to grow. Let go of your human attempts to walk and let God move you.

Fourth, you who have sinned and recognize your need for God to cleanse your heart and restore your standing with Him. Let God wash away your sin and renew your heart.

Finally, you who have a disability or, for that matter, any problem that hinders you. It may be physical, emotional, or mental. In any case, those who need a tool to help you get through anything.

My prayer is that all of you listen to my words; that my words would reveal the truth that you are weak and powerless and in need of help from God; that the truth would lead you to allow God to help in every facet of your life. And that with God's help, life can be all it was intended to be. See the truth. Follow the truth. Live the truth.

◆ ◆ ◆

Editors Note: Aaron Gunzer never saw his book published. An email on February 2007 from his brother Jason, read:

"I regret to inform you that Aaron Gunzer passed away on February 14 at 1:30 P.M. He went suddenly, painlessly, and peacefully. One minute he was fine, and the next he was in heaven. It's good to know that we know where he is, and that he left a legacy: his book."

Aaron was 28 years old.

References

1. Internet: http:geocities.com/HotSprings/Spa/9599/Theodore.html.
2. Internet: http:sermon illustrator.org/illustrator/sermon3b/revised version of Psalm 23.
3. “Our Great Savior” by J. Wilbur Chapman
4. Peter Marshall, *Mr. Jones Meets the Master* (New York: Fleming H. Revell, 1950, 2nd ed.), pp. 147-48
5. Author Unknown
6. Internet: http:people.howstuffworks.com/laughter

978-0-595-45481-
0-595-45481-X